CIRCLES OF SORROW, LINES OF STRUGGLE

CIRCLES OF SORROW,

LINES OF STRUGGLE

The Novels of Toni Morrison

GURLEEN GREWAL

LOUISIANA STATE UNIVERSITY PRESS

Baton Rouge

Designer: Amanda McDonald Key
Typeface: Goudy
Typesetter: Wilsted & Taylor Publishing Services

A partial version of chapter 1 appeared in *Approaches to Teaching the Novels of Toni Morrison*, edited by
Nellie McKay and Katherine Earle (New York: MLA of America, 1997). A partial version of chapter 5
appeared in *Memory and Cultural Politics: New Approaches to American Ethnic Literatures*, edited by
Amritjit Singh, Joseph T. Skerrett, Jr., and Robert E. Hogan (Boston: Northeastern University Press, 1996).

Library of Congress Cataloging-in-Publication Data
Grewal, Gurleen.
    Circles of sorrow, lines of struggle: the novels of Toni Morrison
    / Gurleen Grewal.
        p.   cm. — (Southern literary studies)
    Includes bibliographical references (p.) and index.
    ISBN 0-8071-2297-1 (alk. paper)
    1. Morrison, Toni—Criticism and interpretation.   2. Women and
literature—United States—History—20th century.   3. Afro-American
women in literature.   4. Afro-Americans in literature.   I. Title.
II. Series.
PS3563.08749Z655   1998
813'.54—dc21   98-5630
                                                        CIP

For my parents, Jasmer Kaur and Sangat Singh Grewal

and

In memory of Satpreet Grewal,
brother, healer, anam čara,
who blessed my life with his radiance

CONTENTS

I agree with Dana Polan when she denies that literary criticism is "in any way a metaphor for larger struggles" and asserts "rather, it is a place of such struggles." I have chosen to struggle with and alongside the works of Toni Morrison because she, as Gilles Deleuze and Felix Guattari have said of Kafka, "knew how to offer, how to invent this amorous political life."[1]

Toni Morrison speaks to me—and perhaps to many postcolonial scholars who have thought hard about their own colonial inculcation in English literature—when she admits, "Excising the political from the life of the mind is a sacrifice that has proven costly." In choosing to study Toni Morrison's work, I was responding to a specific challenge—"the quest for relevance"—put to me by my own history: a postcolonial education in India culminating with an American Ph.D. in English, an education à la Matthew Arnold, in "the best that has been thought and said." Not surprisingly, I too felt like the young people in Toni Morrison's Nobel acceptance speech who admit, to the griot, "We have no bird in our hands, living or dead." Let me recall their complaint to the old, blind woman, the repository of narrative wisdom: "Is there no context for our lives? No song, no literature, no poem full of vitamins, no history connected to experience that you can pass along to help us start strong?"[2]

In the modern literature of every nation, the novel appears to satisfy the middle-class demand for self-appraisals of identities, both individual and collective. In postcolonial societies this demand is a kind of hunger, one Toni Morrison understood all too well when she said, "Narrative is radical, creating

---

1. Dana Polan, Introduction to Gilles Deleuze and Felix Guattari, *Kafka: Toward A Minor Literature*, trans. Polan (Minneapolis, Minn. 1986), xxiv, xxv.

2. Toni Morrison, *Playing in the Dark: Whiteness and the Literary Imagination* (Cambridge, Mass., 1992), 12; Toni Morrison, *The Nobel Lecture in Literature, 1993* (New York, 1994), 27. The phrase "quest for relevance" is from N'gugi Thiongo's *Decolonizing the Mind: The Politics of Language in African Literature* (Portsmouth, N.H., 1986), 87.

us at the very moment it is being created."[3] Novels such as *The Bluest Eye* show me something I had always suspected but never fully realized, either in the literature I had read or in the ways of reading I had been taught: the saving power of narrative, its capacity to open a door, to point out the fire *and* the fire escape—in short, the profound work that narrative can do for the social collective, and the work that such a narrative in turn demands from us.

Toni Morrison's work, generated in a post–civil rights milieu, anticipates and coincides with the critique of masculinist Eurocentrism in the U.S. academy—a critique launched from several directions: feminist, postcolonial, and poststructuralist. *The Death of Literature*, Alvin Kernan's postmortem report on the old humanist canon of literature, summarizes the old school's troubled awareness that a certain understanding and dissemination of literature has increasingly become impossible. He rues that literature is "'killed' by the unholy trinity, deconstructionists, marxists, feminists, and that other trio of 'women, blacks, and Third World writers.'" Quite so, but the crux of the matter was better stated by Timothy Brennan when he noted that English literary criticism "has refused to place the fact of domination in a comprehensive approach to its literary material, and that becomes impossible when facing the work of those who have not merely visited but lived it."[4]

I have found it useful to pick up the theme of internal colonialism first developed by black historians in the 1970s in order to articulate the postcolonial concerns of Morrison's literary production. The term *postcolonial* is misleading in its temporal implications. It should be more properly understood to imply the legacy of colonialism that is carried and continued into the present. While the structures of that institution appear to be dismantled, the global power differentials upheld by colonialism are still in place. Its discourse continues to mark the bell curves of knowledge produced in academic institutions both within the United States and elsewhere. The collective trauma of colonialism has neither been "worked through" in social identities nor redressed in political economies. It is in this context that the work of decolonization demands an individual and collective response, a social and political engagement. To such work Toni Morrison has committed her entire literary career. "Writing is a certain way of wanting freedom," notes Jean-Paul Sartre. "The 'engaged' writer

3. Morrison, *The Nobel Lecture*, 27.

4. Alvin Kernan, *The Death of Literature* (New Haven, 1990), 3; Timothy Brennan, *Salman Rushdie and the Third World: Myths of the Nation* (New York, 1989), 6.

knows that words are action. He knows that to reveal is to change, and that one can reveal only by planning to change."[5] This impulse to reveal/educate/ change is consistently present in Toni Morrison's work and accounts for much of its emotive force.

Literary critic Harold Bloom confesses that he "reread[s] Morrison because her imagination, *whatever her social purposes*, transcends ideology and polemics, and enters again into the literary space occupied only by fantasy and romance of authentic aesthetic dignity." I would posit, however, that Morrison's work does not transcend ideology; indeed, the following essays attempt to close the tiresome gap between the "aesthetic" and the "ideological" in interpreting her novels. If Morrison's writing makes aesthetic sense to the reader, it is not in spite of but because of the ideological vision propelling that art. Good writing, as Terry Eagleton explains, "also means having at one's disposal an ideological perspective which can penetrate to the realities of [human] experience in a certain situation."[6] I am indebted to the historical materialist feminist tradition (that goes back to Raymond Williams and beyond), from which we learn that the literary text is not isolated but embedded in and constituted by the material and historical processes to which it belongs, processes upon which the literary text may exert its own radical longings and determinations.

What we make of these literary determinations is another story. "Make me, remake me," says the unseen narrator in *Jazz*. And in that making and remaking of meaning comes a different kind of emergency, for it is also *we* who are being remade by the text—reading becomes a profoundly pedagogic process of leading and being led. At the end of the Nobel speech, itself a virtuoso pedagogic performance (*pedagogue*: one who leads a child), the griot says: "I trust you now. I trust you now with the bird that is not in your hands because you have truly caught it. Look. How lovely it is, this thing we have done—together."[7] The narrative of lack and plenitude, of love and outrage, is registered in the collaborative social space of teller and listener, writer and reader. In that space, we are entrusted with nothing less than the trust of the word/world urging us to make it, remake it.

Alas, this book must go to press without including *Paradise*, Toni Morrison's

5. Jean-Paul Sartre, *What Is Literature?* (New York, 1966), 42, 14.

6. Harold Bloom, Introduction to *Toni Morrison*, ed. Bloom (New York, 1990), 2, italics mine; Terry Eagleton, *Marxism and Literary Criticism* (Berkeley, 1976), 8.

7. Toni Morrison, *Jazz* (New York, 1992), 229; Morrison, *The Nobel Lecture*, 30.

latest novel completing her Dante-like trilogy, begun with the inferno of *Beloved* and sequeled by the purgatorial realm of *Jazz*. I am grateful that her work goes on. During the long journey of writing the essays that follow, I found Morrison a profound teacher, a healer whose medium is the word, and whose terrain is nothing less than the collective *karma* of generations and its reverberations and transformations in time. Musicians, healers and wise storytellers know that words have resonances that go beyond the outer ear. Although I did not consciously recognize this when I began a decade ago, my inner listening responded to the ensouled nature of Morrison's voice, and it has been a pleasure to grow and understand life's complexities alongside her books.

At this juncture, W. S. Mervin speaks well for me:

it has taken me till now
to be able to say
even this
it has taken me this long
to know what I cannot say.

. . . .

Beginning
I am here
please
be ready to teach me
I am almost ready to learn.[8]

This book is dedicated to my beloved parents, Sangat Singh and Jasmer Kaur, who gave me what they themselves did without, and for always doing the best they could. Sadly, this book must now commemorate my brother Satpreet Grewal, who understood the circles of sorrow and cut through them on January 1, 1998. This book, and so much else in my life, would not have been possible without his healing presence and compassionate wisdom buoying me through the years. I thank Satpreet for giving me that most rare gift, unconditional love. Friends and family join me in thanking him for his exceptional work as a homeopath and teacher, listener, counselor. His blessings continue to blossom in his absence.

Over the years of working on this book, I have become indebted to many

8. W. S. Merwin, "The Piper," in his *The Second Four Books of Poems* (Port Townsend, Wash., 1993), 151–52.

friends, colleagues, and teachers. Among them I would like to thank Barbara Christian for the stimulating discussions of black women's literature and for her encouragement at a time I most needed it; Abdul JanMohamed for challenging me to think further; Linda Morris and Michael Hoffman for their firm support of this project in its early stages at the University of California, Davis; and Lata Mani for spurring my own rethinking of feminist history. I also thank my genial and supportive colleagues in the women's studies department at the University of South Florida.

Written in Davis and Berkeley, California, and completed in Tampa, Florida, this book has been furthered by a grant from the Division of Sponsored Research at the University of South Florida, Tampa, which I acknowledge with many thanks. At Louisiana State University Press, my thanks go especially to John Easterly for his infinite patience with the manuscript. I'm grateful, too, to Fred Hobson, editor of the Press's Southern Literary Studies series. And I thank Donna Perreault and Sarah Richards Doerries for being terrific editors.

This acknowledgement would be incomplete without a word of appreciation to the circle of kindred spirits who, at various stages, and in their own different ways, tempered the lines of struggle: Margaret Bedrosian, Hema Chari, Renate Dohmen, Kirsten Fischer, M. Javed, Shreeram Krishnaswamy, Amitava Kumar, Maggie McClain, Deepika Petraglia-Bahri, Beheroze Shroff, and Kurt Van Wilt. I thank all my teachers at Indraprastha College for Women, Delhi, and all my dear friends from Indraprastha, Davis, and Tampa who continue to offer the sustenance of friendship. My gratitude extends especially to Freny Khodaiji for being herself at all times, to Shernaz Italia for providing me another home at K-45, and to Bhavana Ganatra for understanding without words. I also thank Olu Oguibe for being there.

Finally, I offer heartfelt thanks to Herleen Kailey for her wonderful spirit and for all the years of sisterhood. And the same to Srini Narayanan, whose caring friendship, encouragement, and understanding over the years supported the work of this book.

INTRODUCTION

Freeing yourself was one thing, claiming ownership of
that freed self was another.
                              —Toni Morrison

Social relations are not only received; they are also
made and can be transformed.
                              —Raymond Williams

Toni Morrison is part of a long black—and American—literary tradition
that finds its full and complicated bloom in her art. Her novels are multivoiced,
multilayered, writerly and speakerly, both popular and literary highbrow. In
her writing the confluence of two streams of narrative tradition is made visible
and audible: one the oral tradition of storytelling passed down over generations
in her own family and community, custodians of a history far removed from
the world of the bourgeois novel, whose narrative tradition is the other Morrison appropriates. At Cornell Morrison studied the stylists of modernist memory, Virginia Woolf and William Faulkner, both of whom had cracked open
the novel to observe more intimately the secular processes of fragmentation
and madness. After them, Morrison takes the novel home to the intimate
address of the rural and urban African American tradition from which she
came, back to the blues with its longstanding tradition of voicing pain, registering complaint and comfort. The unrelenting lyrical pressure of her prose
aims to unsettle as well as to heal. It charges us with nothing less than the
charge of history; her characters, though seldom in powerful social positions,
command their desires in an outlawed agency that puts into crisis the law of
the land and the judgment of the witnessing jury of readers.

A powerful catalyst for Morrison's work—one so ubiquitous it can escape notice—is what Howard Winant calls the "pervasive crisis of race" facing the contemporary United States: "a crisis no less severe than those of the past. The origins of the crisis are not particularly obscure: the cultural and political meaning of race, its significance in shaping the social structure, and its experiential or existential dimensions all remain profoundly unresolved as the United States approaches the end of the twentieth century. As a result, the society as a whole and the population as individuals suffer from confusion and anxiety about the issue (or complex of issues) we call race." Morrison has increasingly committed herself to addressing issues of race outside her own fiction. Her unpublished drama *Dreaming Emmett*, produced in 1985 to "commemorate the first celebration of the Rev. Dr. Martin Luther King Jr.'s birthday as a national holiday," was written in response to the 1955 racist killing in Mississippi of a fourteen-year-old black boy named Emmett Till; the play was "intended to symbolize the plight of contemporary black urban youth—their disproportionately high rate of death by violence." In *Playing in the Dark: Whiteness and the Literary Imagination*, a work of literary criticism, Toni Morrison undertakes the task of showing that "Africanism is inextricable from the definition of Americanness—from its origins on through its integrated or disintegrated twentieth-century self." In the national canonical literature, Morrison discovers "a sometimes allegorical, sometimes metaphorical, but always choked representation of an Africanist presence." *Playing in the Dark* thus brings to light the various roles played by "the thunderous, theatrical presence of black surrogacy" in the construction of whiteness in the nation's literary imagination.[1]

In assessing the phenomenon of Toni Morrison, we need to keep in mind "the pressures and limits of the social relationships on which as a producer, the author depends"—what Raymond Williams calls "the political economy of writing." We need to take into account the demand for and the reception of writings by black women following the civil rights movement. The contemporary literary renaissance started in 1965 with Margaret Walker's *Jubilee* and Paule Marshall's *The Chosen Place, The Timeless People* and took off in 1970

---

1. Howard Winant, "Postmodern Racial Politics in the United States: Difference and Inequality," *Socialist Review* (January–March, 1990), 121; Margaret Croyden, "Toni Morrison Tries Her Hand at Playwriting," in *Conversations with Toni Morrison*, ed. Danille Taylor-Guthrie (Jackson, Miss., 1994), 218, 220; Morrison, *Playing in the Dark*, 65, 117, 13.

with Toni Morrison's *The Bluest Eye*, Toni Cade's edition of *The Black Woman*, Alice Walker's *The Third Life of Grange Copeland*, and Maya Angelou's *I Know Why the Caged Bird Sings*. Since the 1970s, we have witnessed a remarkable efflorescence. Toni Morrison herself has played an active role in promoting black voices. As editor at Random House, she ensured that black writers would find a receptive space in publishing, that the integrity of their voices would not be compromised by the imposition of alien standards. A host of important black publications (by authors such as Mohammed Ali, Toni Cade Bambara, Angela Davis, and Gayl Jones) have received Morrison's encouragement. It is important to note that this profusion of creative expression has been aided by a "community of cultural workers" that includes black feminist critics and teachers of literature whose receptive work shows, in Hortense Spillers' words, that "traditions are not born. They are made." A tradition "arises not only because there are writers there to make it, but also because there is a strategic audience of heightened consciousness prepared to read and interpret the work as such." Unlike their literary foremothers, writers like Toni Morrison and Alice Walker had sturdy black bridges already made for them. Their works paralleled the energy generated by the black cultural and political mobilization of the 1960s and 1970s and the black feminist resurgence of the 1980s. In what is now a landmark essay, "Toward a Black Feminist Criticism," Barbara Smith writes, "A viable, autonomous black feminist movement in this country would open up the space needed for the exploration of black women's lives and the creation of consciously black woman-identified art."[2]

Toni Morrison's feminism partakes of the black cultural resistance to liberal white feminism. In "What the Black Woman Thinks about Women's Lib," she notes that the different histories, and therefore agendas, of white and black women are made apparent in bathroom signs designating "White Ladies" and "Colored Women." Morrison refers to the conflictual power relationship between the white *lady* and the colored *woman* in several of her works: in the relationship between Pauline Breedlove and Mrs. Fisher in *The Bluest Eye*; First Corinthians and her poet-mistress Michael Mary Graham in *Song of Solomon*;

2. Raymond Williams, *Marxism and Literature* (Oxford, 1977), 193; Hortense J. Spillers, "Afterword: Cross-Currents, Discontinuities: Black Women's Fiction," *Conjuring: Black Women's Fiction, and Literary Tradition*, ed. Hortense Spillers and Marjorie Pryse (Bloomington, Ind., 1985), 250; Barbara Smith, "Toward a Black Feminist Criticism," in *Feminist Criticism and Social Change*, ed. Judith Newton and Deborah Rosenfelt (New York, 1985), 4.

Ondine and her young mistress Margaret in *Tar Baby*; Sethe and her owner, Mrs. Garner, in *Beloved*; Vera Louise and True Belle in *Jazz*. Alice Walker joins Morrison in disclaiming bourgeois white feminism by claiming under the name *womanist* a feminism appropriate to the historical experience and needs of black women.[3] While a black feminist point of view is clearly evident in Toni Morrison's work, it is always contextual and relational, articulated with respect to issues of class and community. While the white-identified individualism of her male and female bourgeois characters is historicized and located within social relations of power and desire, narrative affect is usually on the side of those who are subordinated to bourgeois power.

Historically, the novel is an art form pertaining to the interests and values of the middle class. Morrison says her writing "bears witness" for a middle-class black audience: "I agree with John Berger that peasants don't write novels because they don't need them. They have a portrait of themselves from gossip, tales, music, and some celebrations. That is enough. . . . Now my people, we 'peasants,' have come to the city, that is to say, we live with its values. There is a confrontation between old values of the tribes and new urban values. It's confusing." In another interview Morrison returns to this theme: "when the peasant class, or lower class, or what have you, confronts the middle class, the city, or the upper classes, they are thrown a little bit into disarray." Toni Morrison's novels tend the gap between emergent middle-class black America and its subaltern origins: she has called her work "peasant literature for *my* people." Susan Willis situates black women's writing, Morrison's included, in the historical transition from an agrarian to an urban society. She makes the important point that "migration to the North signifies more than a confrontation with (and contamination by) the white world. It implies a transition in social class." Morrison is a writer with a firm grasp of the lived dynamics of class experience, a subject that has received less critical attention by feminist scholars than the issue of gender. Drawing on experiences as varied as those of her grandparents' southern rural life to her parents' small-town existence in the Midwest to her own life, which includes the cosmopolitan ethos of New York City, Morrison is able to command in her fiction a century's experience

---

3. Morrison, "What the Black Woman Thinks About Women's Lib," *New York Times Magazine*, August 22, 1971, p. 15; Alice Walker, *In Search of Our Mothers' Gardens* (New York, 1983), xi.

of change affecting African Americans. Wilfred Sheed's observation of Morrison's range of understanding is apt: "Most black writers are privy, like the rest of us, to bits and pieces of the secret, the dark side of their group experience, but Toni Morrison uniquely seems to have all the keys on her chain, like a house detective. . . . She [has] the run of the whole place, from ghetto to small town to ramshackle farmhouse, to bring back a panorama of black myth and reality that [dazzles] the senses."[4]

Morrison's novels may be read as anti-*Bildung* projects that subvert dominant middle-class ideology. *The Bluest Eye,* an indictment of racism, is also a stinging critique of an educated class of blacks who, in order to avail themselves of the bourgeois privileges of a capitalist economy, have made "individuals" of themselves. The three uneducated whores shunned by the town's respectable folk are presented more favorably than the educated Geraldine and Soaphead Church, whose complicity earns authorial contempt even as it requires our understanding. In *Sula,* the middle-class, color-conscious Helene Wright is treated with much less affection than the lesser-privileged Eva and Hannah Peace. *Song of Solomon*'s Milkman Dead, an individualist raised and trapped in the self-centered, bourgeois world of the middle-class nuclear family, has to be rescued from under the myopic vision of his genteel mother and petit-bourgeois father. The rescue is effected by his Aunt Pilate, a peasant woman who even in her isolation and marginality is endowed with formidable strength arising from her nonbourgeois identity. *Tar Baby* inscribes a greater sympathy for the vagabond son of the soil, Son Green, than for the upper-middle-class individualist, Jadine Childs. In an interview in 1981, Morrison shed light on the authorial resentment of Jadine: "There is a new, capitalistic, modern American black which is what everybody thought was the ultimate in integration. To produce Jadine, that's what it was for. I think there is some danger in the result of that production."[5] In *Jazz,* Joe Trace is not the New Negro of Alain Locke and the talented tenth of the Harlem Renaissance. The New Negro is the migrant peasant who died so many times he could not help being made new.

---

4. Toni Morrison, "The Language Must Not Sweat," Interview with Thomas LeClair in *Conversations,* 120, 121; Toni Morrison, "Rootedness: The Ancestor as Foundation," in *Black Women Writers at Work, 1950–1980,* ed. Mari Evans (Garden City, N.Y., 1984), 340; Susan Willis, *Specifying: Black Women Writing the American Experience* (Madison, Wis., 1987), 83–109; Wilfred Sheed, "Improbable Assignment: *Tar Baby,*" *Atlantic* (April, 1981), 119.

5. Morrison, interview with Charles Ruas, in *Conversations,* 105.

Thus an identity claimed by the privileged few—the educated cosmopolitan elite—is problematized and revised from the perspective of those who had no access to the bourgeois modes of self-making.

In an interview Morrison said that "black people have always been used as a buffer in this country between powers to prevent class war, to prevent other kinds of real conflagrations":

If there were no black people here in this country, it would have been Balkanized. The immigrants would have torn each other's throats out, as they have done everywhere else. But in becoming an American, from Europe, what one has in common with that other immigrant is contempt for *me*—it's nothing less but color. Wherever they were from, they would stand together. They could all say, "I am not *that*." So in that sense, becoming an American is based on an attitude: an exclusion of me. . . . It wasn't negative to them—it was unifying. When they got off the boat, the second word they learned was "nigger." . . . Every immigrant knew he would not come at the very bottom. He had to come above at least one group—and that was us.

However, the idea that others have constructed their unity through being nonblack does not imply that being black, in turn, promotes unity. In fact, the colonial policy of racialization (in which color lines organized class hierarchy) did not facilitate the formation of a collectivity. The very idea of collectivity is something that must be imagined or created, the divisions historicized and understood; it must be narrated or performed. As Benedict Anderson observed, this collective self-composition is the creative project of nationalism. In the case of Afro-America, where nationalism has literally no *ground* of its own, the project of nationalism or counternationalism becomes of necessity a cultural one. As Wahneema Lubiano notes, the question of black nationhood implies "the activation of a narrative of identity and interest" against the history of the U.S. state; it is a discourse that "functions as a defense against cultural imperialism."[6]

Internationally, Toni Morrison is part of a growing body of contemporary writers who are responding to imperatives of cultural critique, reclamation, and redefinition—imperatives broadly termed *postcolonial*. Helen Tiffin defines the

6. Toni Morrison, qtd. in Bonnie Angelo, "The Pain of Being Black," *Time*, May 22, 1989, p. 120; Wahneema Lubiano, in a paper on black cultural nationalism delivered at the Modern Language Association Convention (New York, 1992).

"dis/mantling, de/mystification and unmasking of European authority" along with the endeavour to "define a denied or outlawed self" as one of the main decolonizing endeavors of postcolonial literatures. N'gugi defines decolonization as a "quest for relevance" wherein the emphasis is interior, directed toward postcolonial society rather than outwardly toward the colonizer. Morrison's creative project has an affinity with the work of decolonization undertaken by Nigerian novelist Chinua Achebe. Although they are very different writers, note what Achebe considers "an adequate revolution for [him] to espouse" in his writing: "to help my society regain belief in itself and put away the complexes of the years of denigration and self-abasement. And it is essentially a question of education, in the best sense of the word. Here, I think my aims and the deepest aspirations of my society meet. For no thinking African can escape the pain of the wound in our soul."[7]

In her essay "Subaltern Studies in a U.S. Frame," Eva Cherniavsky notes that "a postcolonial approach to U.S. history and culture would speak to the contradictions of a naturalized/nationalized colonial domination," one that "systematically displaces both indigenous peoples and nonwhite labor from the social and symbolic territory of the consensual Euro-American state."[8] Just as the wealth and labor of the colonies consolidated the identity of Western Europe, so the colonized land of Native Americans and the colonized labor of African Americans provided the early cohesion of the nation of *immigrants*, a term that is itself part of an obfuscating nationalist vocabulary.

The term *domestic* (or *internal*) *colonialism* was developed by black historians in the 1960s and early 1970s to refer to the experience of black people in America. The theory of internal colonialism situates the African slave trade within the expansionist demands of Euro-American capitalism. According to Robert Allen, "the most profound conclusion to be drawn from a survey of the black experience in America [is] to consider Black America as a semi-colony." Social critic Harold Cruse explains it thus: "The only factor which differentiates the Negro's status from that of a pure colonial status is that his position is maintained in the 'home' country in close proximity to the dominant racial group." Black feminist scholars such as Hazel Carby, Patricia Hill Collins, and

7. Helen Tiffin, "Post-Colonialism, Post-Modernism and the Rehabilitation of Post-Colonial History," *Journal of Commonwealth Literature*, XXIII (1988), 171; Thiongo, *Decolonizing the Mind*, 87; Chinua Achebe, *Hopes and Impediments: Selected Essays* (New York, 1988), 44.

8. Eva Cherniavsky, "Subaltern Studies in a U.S. Frame," *Boundary 2*, XXIII (1996), 85–110.

Angela Davis have documented the various ways in which black women served the model of white womanhood by filling the role of the "self-consolidating Other" (Gayatri Spivak's succinct phrase). In a similar vein, Toni Morrison's *Playing in the Dark* examines the national shadow play wherein an unacknowledged blackness inheres in and constitutes white identity and unity, and spurs the anxiety that underlies the accomplished national persona of a *"new white man"* in the writings of Hawthorne, Melville, Twain, Poe, and others.[9] In the tradition of postcolonial writing and criticism, Morrison rewrites the nation from a perspective committed to what has been excised. Her novels mean to revise dominant historiography, reconsidering the scene of colonial violation from the inside, from subaltern perspectives hitherto ignored.

Morrison's literary project involves confronting the national chasms of race, class, and gender as they are lived by individuals. A cursory glance at some of the epigraphs of her novels clarifies the nature of the problems Morrison tackles in her work. The epigraph of *Song of Solomon* pursues the subject of liberating a suppressed identity: "The fathers may soar / And the children may know their names," and that of *Tar Baby* acknowledges the difficulty of a postcolonial solidarity: "For it hath been declared / unto me of you, my brethren . . . that there are contentions among you." Solidarity can best be established on the collective ground of past oppression, as evident in both the dedication of *Beloved*, for "Sixty Million / and more," and its epigraph, "I will call them my people, / which were not my people; / and her beloved, / which was not beloved." As the epigraph to *Jazz* indicates, Morrison's novels may be read as a designation of divisions and a prodigious attempt to historicize them. Satya Mohanty's comment about *Beloved* illuminates what is at stake in a postcolonial return to the archives: "[*Beloved*] is one of the most challenging of postcolonial texts because it indicates the extent to which the search for a genuinely noncolonial moral and cultural identity depends on a revisionary historiography. We cannot really claim ourselves morally or politically until we have reconstructed our collective identity, reexamined our dead and our disremembered. The project is not simply one of adding to one's ancestral line, for . . . it involves fundamental

9. Robert Allen, *Black Awakening in Capitalist America* (Garden City, N.Y., 1970), 2; Harold Cruse, *Rebellion or Revolution?* (New York, 1968), 76–77; Gayatri Chakravarty Spivak, "Rani of Sirmur," in *Europe and Its Others: Proceedings of the Essex Conference on the Sociology of Literature, July, 1984*, ed. Francis Barker, *et al.* (2 vols.; Colchester, Eng., 1985), I, 130; Morrison, *Playing in the Dark, passim.*

discoveries about what ancestry is, what continuity consists in, how cultural meanings do not just sustain themselves through history but are in fact materially embodied and fought for." *Beloved* allows us to see that a revisionary postcolonial historiography must also be feminist. As Kumkum Sangari and Sudesh Vaid have insisted, it must "acknowledg[e] that each aspect of reality is gendered," and that it "may be feminist without being, exclusively, women's history."[10]

For Morrison, language implies agency—"an act with consequences." The first sentence of Morrison's Nobel speech addressed to the members of the Swedish academy is, "Ladies and Gentlemen: Narrative has never been merely entertainment for me."[11] Given the context of cultural and political domination, we can appreciate why storytelling assumes such a critical function in both African American and Native American literature, why in Leslie Marmon Silko's novel *Ceremony* we are told:

[Stories] aren't just entertainment.
Don't be fooled.
. . . .
You don't have anything
if you don't have the stories.

As Raymond Williams argues, literature is part of "a whole social process, which, as it is lived, is not only process but is an active history, made up of the realities of formation and of struggle."[12] Toni Morrison's contemporary fiction self-consciously takes its place in the continuum of sociopolitical struggle that has historically characterized African American experience.

In their discussion of Kafka's writing, Gilles Deleuze and Felix Guattari coin the term *minor literature* to denote "that which a minority constructs out of a major language." Far from denoting a diminutive function, it is "the glory" of minor literature "to be the revolutionary force for all literature." In its salient

10. Satya Mohanty, "The Epistemic Status of Cultural Identity: On *Beloved* and the Postcolonial Condition," *Cultural Critique*, XXIV (Spring, 1993), 67; Kumkum Sangari and Sudesh Vaid, qtd. in R. Radhakrishnan, "Nationalism, Gender, and the Narrative of Identity," in *Nationalisms and Sexualities*, ed. Andrew Parker, Mary Russo, *et al.* (New York, 1992), 79.

11. Morrison, *The Nobel Lecture*.

12. Williams, *Marxism and Literature*, 210.

features they see the conditions of all revolutionary literature: "the deterritorialization of language, the connection of the individual to a political immediacy, and the collective assemblage of enuniciation."[13] Deleuze and Guattari's assertions invite testing in relation to the works of Toni Morrison, who constructs her African American literary worlds out of the major language of English, just as Kafka, a Czech Jew, deterritorialized high German.

Morrison certainly deterritorializes the English language. Entering the bourgeois aesthetic field of the Anglo-American novel, Morrison appropriates classical and biblical myths and the canonical writings of high modernism and places them in the matrix of black culture. In this she is supported by the long vernacular tradition of work songs, spirituals, and blues that had already appropriated the Bible and renamed the Israelites as the people chosen from Africa. Morrison's own practice of naming not only deterritorializes Anglo-European usage, it signifies on its history—consider the biblical names in *Song of Solomon*, or *Jazz* with its southern towns of Wordsworth, Troy, Vienna, and Rome. What makes this appropriation so impressive is the claim made on the unyielding land by African American desire—the force that breaks through the liminality of a history of suffering, enlarging the space of marginality until it opens out into the entire field of history on its own terms.

A second characteristic that marks minor literatures is that "everything in them is political. In major literatures, in contrast, the individual concern (familial, marital, and so on) joins with other no less individual concerns, the social milieu serving as a mere environment or a background. . . . Minor literature is completely different; its cramped space forces each individual intrigue to connect immediately to politics. The individual concern thus becomes all the more necessary, indispensable, because a whole other story is vibrating within it."[14] Minor literature, in other words, constructs a different discourse, whose burden is to challenge dominant ideologies and representations by claiming an alternative epistemological and ethical space. The social milieu cannot serve as a mere background—and it never does in Morrison's work—because what is at stake in minor literature is precisely the reconstitution of an untenable social milieu; it aims to reorient the reader's relationship to an existing reality by foregrounding the environment.

A third feature Deleuze and Guattari observe in minor literatures is that

13. Deleuze and Guattari, *Toward a Minor Literature*, 16, 19, 18.
14. *Ibid.*, 17.

"everything takes on a collective value." Because collective consciousness is not operant "in external life," or "the conditions of a collective enunciation" are absent, "literature finds itself positively charged with the role and function of collective, and even revolutionary, enunciation": "it is literature that produces an active solidarity in spite of skepticism and if the writer is in the margins or completely outside his or her fragile community, this situation allows the writer all the more the possibility to express another possible community and to forge the means for another consciousness and another sensibility."[15] In novels such as *The Bluest Eye, Sula, Beloved,* and *Jazz,* a localized individual concern—Pecola's problem, Sula's heresy, Sethe's haunting, Joe and Violet's violence—sets into motion a dialogic of memory in which the individual concern is decentered and becomes the enunciation of the collective.

A fourth significant characteristic of minor literature is that it makes language "vibrate with a new intensity" partly deriving from *"terms that connote pain."* Deleuze and Guattari refer to "an intensive utilization [of language] that makes it take flight along creative lines of escape," "us[ing] syntax in order to cry, to give a syntax to the cry."[16] One of the most remarkable elements of Morrison's prose is the sensational or visceral evocation of pain; its power stems from the author's ability to translate the experience of political inequities and wrongs with lyrical effect.

Toni Morrison's fiction makes us reevaluate individuals via the complex sociopolitical history that bespeaks them. Her novels aim to redistribute the pressure of accountability from the axis of the individual to that of the collective. Her art draws its imperatives from personal and collective histories: the maternal and paternal inheritance of a working-class consciousness with southern roots; the black aesthetic movement of the 1960s with its reclamation of oral traditions of storytelling and folk music as authentic modes of cultural expression; the liberation narrative of black history itself. As an African American novelist within the American literary tradition, Morrison interrogates national identity and reconstructs social memory. It is a truism of contemporary understanding that public identity is the product of nationalism, whose work it is to link a people dispersed by difference to a common past. As historians such as Benedict Anderson have pointed out, this common past is not simply there to

15. *Ibid.,* 17.
16. *Ibid.,* 22, 26 (authors' emphasis).

access but is made available by imagined or constructed narratives of the nation. However—and this is a central question Morrison's work addresses—what happens to the identity of a group within a nation built upon its marginalization? Further, in what ways can a marginalized identity construct its own knowledge? What new modes of narration are required to voice its presence? It is not surprising that Toni Morrison's literary project has affinities with the tasks of historiography. Writing the past, in historian Michael Roth's words, "is one of the crucial vehicles for reconstructing or reimagining a community's connections to its traditions. This is especially true for groups who have been excluded from the mainstream national histories that have dominated Western historiography, and who have suffered a weakening of group memory as part of their experience of modernity."[17]

Morrison's project of remembering must be appreciated in the context of the privatization of individual memory. As Michael Roth notes, "memory in modernity is seen less as a public, collective function than as a private, psychological faculty: it is imagined by philosophers and doctors from the eighteenth century on as being internal to each of us, at the core of the psychological self. We are what we remember. . . . But the psychologization of memory makes it extremely difficult for people to share the past, for them to have confidence that they have a collective connection to what has gone before." In Morrison's novels memory "becomes a locus of struggle over the boundary between the individual and the collective." The novels exploit the idiosyncratic compositions of individual memory, the unique particularities of personal reminiscence, only to re-collect them in the frame of a larger, unfolding history. Michael Lambek and Paul Antze observed that "the rise of popular therapeutic discourse in North America has gone hand in hand with widespread political disengagement." As they succinctly put it, "historical trauma is displaced by individual drama," resulting in "a shift in moral focus from collective obligations to narratives of individual suffering."[18] Morrison means to reverse this pattern. As her various characters attest, their lives do not make sense outside history: the meaning of personal suffering is available only within a collective temporality.

17. Benedict Anderson, *Imagined Communities: Reflections on the Origin and Spread of Nationalism* (New York, 1983); Michael Roth, *The Ironist's Cage: Memory, Trauma, and the Construction of History* (New York, 1995), 10.

18. Roth, *The Ironist's Cage*, 9; Paul Antze and Michael Lambek, eds. *Tense Past: Cultural Essays in Trauma and Memory* (New York, 1996), xx, xxiv.

The post-Faulknerian American novel is of a genre that allows for the detailed exploration of interiority—a hallmark of Morrison's fiction, with its array of characters the reader comes to know with astonishing intimacy. In fact, Morrison's appeal and achievement lies in her ability to create individuals, with all their idiosyncracies, while anchoring subjectivity *in a collective history* without which it would have little meaning. This achievement stems from an ideological position not readily available from the position of bourgeois individualism. As Kumkum Sangari notes, "Individuality is a truly connective definition—that which connects the subject to a collectivity—so that it is the richness of contextualization that *sets off* the notion of personal particularity and differentiates the individual, rather than the social collectivity itself as being subject to the unique perception of the bourgeois individual." Morrison pays a great deal of attention to individual consciousness; we are made to see what constitutes a particular character's subjectivity and what diminishes or augments the humanity of that character. But in that appraisal Morrison compels us to evaluate not just the individual but the entire complex sociopolitical history that constitutes the individual. What Toni Morrison said in 1976 of Gayl Jones's first novel, *Corregidora,* is most applicable to her own work: what "accounts for the success" is "the weight of history working itself out in the life of one, two, three people: I mean a large idea, brought down small, and at home, which gives it a universality and a particularity which makes it extraordinary."[19]

Morrison's novels allow us to examine the quality of human relationships under the constraints of historical processes and social relations, in the context of a collective. The emphasis on the interiority of her characters, the acknowledgment and enactment of desire in all its unruly forms, becomes a way of countering the diminishing of the subordinated, alienated self. Morrison remarked in a television interview that people often say her characters appear larger than life; she countered that they are "*as* large as life, not larger. Life *is* large."[20] That individuals' large desires remain unfulfilled or thwarted creates the ambience of loss—a loss that adds powerful affect to the critique of history.

Through the evocation of specific, historicized landscapes of loss and erosion, the reader is made to see in individual loss—usually incurred by exceeding

19. Kumkum Sangari, "Politics of the Possible," *Cultural Critique,* VII (Fall, 1987); Morrison, "Intimate Things in Place," interview with Robert Stepto, in *Conversations,* 29.

20. Toni Morrison, *Toni Morrison,* an RM Arts Production, 1987.

social limits—the limitations of the socius. It is thus that emotions of loss become charged with the intelligence of a critique. By endowing pain—itself mute and inchoate and all too personal—with a narrative that is as intelligible as it is social, Morrison makes room for recovery that is at once cognitive and emotional, therapeutic and political. Loss is both historicized and mourned so that it acquires a collective force and a political understanding. Morrison's fictive circles of sorrow invite readers to become *conscious* of the terrain of their lives, to re-cognize the terrain as not simply individual or personal but as thoroughly social, traversed by the claims of the past, occupied by conflicting ideologies of identity (class, gender, race, nationhood) that give rise to the boundaries of the self. In the novels, the place of the individual is de-isolated, the boundaries of the self shown to be permeated by the collective struggle of historical agents who live the long sentence of history by succumbing to (re-peating), contesting, and remaking it.

Each novel charts a destruction recalled through the mnemonic prisms of multiple characters; the story of destruction and loss becomes a historical and political testimony that we as readers participate in as belated witnesses. As the story of loss is transferred to us, we become its interpreters, collaborating in the work of understanding. Each novel draws us into its circles of sorrow with the imperative to make sense; we do so by yielding our own knowledge of destruction and loss, by struggling alongside the characters. Unlike the healing transference between client and analyst in the consulting room—where the healing is private and concealed—the literary therapeutic narrative is social and collective, opening out into the politics of the world. The strategy of Morrison's novels is always to make sense of the individual psyche and memory in wider social and political terms. As a chronicler of African American ex-perience, Morrison's contribution has been to create, in the face of public dissociation of a painful past, a space where the traumatic material may find a coherent articulation and a collective dimension. Her novels create a "public space of trauma," a space Laurence Kirmayer defined as "provid[ing] a consen-sual reality and collective memory through which the fragments of personal memory can be assembled, reconstructed, and displayed with a tacit assumption of validity." The construction of such a space is all the more urgent given "the failure of the world to bear witness." "The social world fails to bear witness for many reasons. Even reparative accounts of the terrible things that happen to people (violations, traumas, losses) are warded off because of their capacity to to create vicarious fear and pain and because they constitute a threat to social and political arrangements."[21]

The work of recovery in Morrison's fiction entails not only the representation of a knowledge excised from dominant understanding, but also the healing from a history that has visited trauma upon its subjects. The function of collective memory in Toni Morrison's work is political as well as therapeutic. As Roth notes, "In addition to establishing a we-group, claiming a legacy of oppression can enable individuals to work through the traumas of their collective and personal histories. The avoidance of a painful past or the failure to recognize its lasting effects often creates disabling patterns of behavior that only cause further pain." As recent studies of trauma relating to the experience of Holocaust survivors have shown, healing depends on the validation of traumatic events. The traumatized do not heal under suppression (amnesia), although forgetting is a characteristic response to trauma. Trauma's unconscious (pathological) mode of expression is to repeat itself, to reenact in a different guise what has never been redressed or represented. The survivor, in the words of Dori Laub, "is not truly in touch either with the core of his traumatic reality or with the fatedness of its reenactments, and thereby remains entrapped in both." What frees the survivor from this entrapment entails the "therapeutic process . . . of constructing a narrative, of reconstructing a history and essentially, of re-externalizing the event." This is precisely what Toni Morrison does. Shoshana Felman's remarks on literature as testimony clarify the relationships between narrative, history/trauma, and healing that are central to Morrison's writing: "the task of the literary testimony is . . . to open up in that belated witness [the reader] . . . the imaginative capability of perceiving history—what is happening to others—in one's own body, with the power of sight (of insight) usually afforded only by one's own immediate physical involvement."[22] Toni Morrison's highly visceral and sensuous prose effects this immediacy of experience.

21. Laurence Kirmayer, "Landscapes of Memory: Trauma, Narrative, and Dissociation," in *Tense Past*, 190, 192.

22. Roth, *The Ironist's Cage*, 10–11; Dori Laub, "Bearing Witness, or the Vicissitudes of Listening," in *Testimony: Crises of Witnessing in Literature, Psychoanalysis, and History*, ed. Shoshana Felman and Laub (New York, 1991), 69; Felman, "Camus' The Plague, or a Monument to Witnessing," in *Testimony*, 108.

*

Addressing the social changes taking place in Europe in the early part of the twentieth century, Walter Benjamin observed that the useful "art of storytelling is reaching its end because the epic side of truth, wisdom, is dying out." Contrasting the oral tradition of storytelling with the written one of the novel, Benjamin remarked that what is eminently present in the former and missing in the latter is the tale's offering of counsel. For him, this move from oral to written is an organic process in which something is both lost and gained: "nothing would be more fatuous than to want to see in it merely a 'symptom of decay,' let alone a 'modern' symptom. It is, rather, only a concomitant symptom of the secular productive forces of history, a concomitant that has quite gradually removed narrative from the realm of living speech and at the same time is making it possible to see a new beauty in what is vanishing." Similarly, Morrison notes the demise of a grounding world view within urban African American communities dislocated from ancestral wisdom and communal forms of expression. A sense of responsibility and urgency characterizes Morrison's comments: "for larger and larger numbers of black people, this sense of loss has grown, and the deeper the conviction that something valuable is slipping away from us, the more necessary it has become to find some way to hold on to the useful past without blocking off the possibilities of the future." Present in Morrison's expressed need to hold on to certain cultural forms of the past is a framework of cultural domination within which these cultural forms have played an oppositional role. Thus Morrison hopes to have her fiction accomplish/replace "what the music did for blacks": "the music kept us alive, but it's not enough anymore. My people are being devoured."[23]

Morrison's invocation of black music is significant, for it is related to a nonbourgeois consciousness not co-opted by the dominant culture. LeRoi Jones wrote that in the face of "the persistent calls to oblivion made by the mainstream of the society," music "was the one vector out of African culture impossible to eradicate. It signified the existence of an Afro-American, and the existence of an Afro-American culture." The musical consciousness was displaced as integration into white America compelled the marginalization of such cultural forms. Hence, for the middle class to have "gotten 'free' of all the blues tradition"

---

23. Walter Benjamin, *Illuminations*, trans. Harry Zohn, ed. Hannah Arendt (New York, 1968), 87; Toni Morrison, "Rediscovering Black History," *New York Times Magazine*, August 11, 1974, p. 14; Morrison, "The Language Must Not Sweat," 121.

was to have been deprived of a vital sense of connection to the resistant traditions of the past. Paule Marshall's *Praisesong for the Widow* is an eloquent and moving account of a black couple, the Johnsons, who had done just that— "gotten 'free'"—and found they had lost an integral part of themselves. The widowed Avey Johnson recalls the significance of the music that had been abandoned in their haste to leave behind a life of poverty and limitations: "Something vivid and affirming and charged with feeling had been present in the small rituals that had once shaped their lives. . . . Something in those small rites, an ethos they held in common, had reached back beyond her life and beyond Jay's to join them to the vast unknown lineage that had made their being possible." And this link, these connections, heard in the music and in the praisesongs, "had both protected them and put them in possession of a kind of power." They spent their lives in pursuit of a different kind of power, one promised by assimilation, a house in the white suburbs; "running with the blinders on they had allowed that richness, protection and power to slip out." Avey bitterly mourns the loss: "What kind of bargain had they struck?"[24]

Marshall's Jay Johnson has much in common with Morrison's Macon Dead, the patriarch in *Song of Solomon* who is driven to amass worldly goods with a compulsion born of the insecurity of dispossession. In a scene of nostalgic hearkening, Macon Dead stands hidden outside his sister Pilate's home, his head pressed to the window, watching and listening as Pilate sings the blues with her daughter and granddaughter, Reba and Hagar. His distance from that setting becomes the measure of his own cultural and spiritual alienation. Hagar demonstrates what Morrison means when she claims, "the music kept us alive, but it's not enough anymore." Hagar is easy prey to an urban consumer culture, a world in which Pilate's song is muted and her wisdom marginalized. Hence Morrison's emphatic statement: "There has to be a mode to do what the music did for blacks." Historically, these expressive cultural forms have been means of forging a collective black consciousness, of keeping alive an awareness of oppression and resistance, of soul force. In wanting her novels to perform the function of black music, Morrison intends her art to forge a historical consciousness, to embody and create a communal intersubjectivity.

In the following passage from *The Bluest Eye*, Morrison reveals something about her own craft: "The pieces of Cholly's life could become coherent only

---

24. LeRoi Jones, *Blues People* (New York, 1963), 131, 176; Paule Marshall, *Praisesong for the Widow* (New York, 1983) 137, 139.

in the head of a musician. Only those who talk their talk through the gold of curved metal, or in the touch of black and white rectangles and taut skins . . . would know how to connect the heart of a red water melon to the asafetida bag . . . to the fists of money to the lemonade in a mason jar . . . and come up with what all of that meant in joy, in pain, in anger, in love, and give it its final and pervading ache of freedom." Words seek to accomplish the emotive-cognitive resonance belonging to music; what we audition in Morrison's novels is the "pervading ache of freedom." This ache accounts for what in Morrison's prose might appear as linguistic extravagance. This pervading ache is "the insistent pressure of *freedom* as the *absent horizon*"—the point Kumkum Sangari made regarding Gabriel García Márquez's narratives, in which absent freedom is "precisely that which is made present and possible by its absence—the lives that people have never lived *because* of the lives they are forced to live or have chosen to live. That which is desired and that which exists, the sense of abundance and the sense of waste, are dialectically related."[25]

In Toni Morrison's art we witness the lyric gesture and force of a minor literature doing the difficult work of decolonization, demystification, and social redress within the dominant language. In attempting to account for the compelling power of this particular literature, I want to add the word *soul,* the dimension least theorized in literary criticism and more acknowledged in music. Toni Morrison is one of the most soulful literary soloists of our time. Explaining the "emotional substance" of jazz, Paul Berliner makes the following comment: "Part and parcel of originality and taste is a performance's 'soul,' its 'spirituality,' its 'integrity of expression.' . . . Soulful performances embody such affective qualities as pathos, intensity, urgency, fire, and energy. . . . Musicians use the term *energy* both literally and figuratively. Just as it requires energy to produce and project sounds on musical instruments, it requires energy for performers to draw upon feelings as they infuse sounds with emotion. Moreover, the sound waves themselves comprise a form of energy that touches listeners physically, potentially also touching them emotionally." Morrison inscribes her own awareness of the energetic properties of sound; consider these lines from *Beloved:* the singing "voices of women searched for the right combination, the key, the code, the sound that broke the back of words. Building voice upon voice until they found it, and when they did it was a wave of sound wide enough to sound deep water and knock the pods off chestnut trees. It broke over Sethe

25. Sangari, "Politics of the Possible," 176.

and she trembled like the baptized in its wash." The dimension of sound in language is potentially a musical or harmonic dimension, an ethereal register in which even the written voice can sing. Here, I can do no more than acknowledge that harmonic dimension in Toni Morrison's prose; its source is the spiritual principle of liberation that animates her writing, a principle I have attempted to elucidate here in its historic, social, and political terms.[26]

26. Paul Berliner, *Thinking in Jazz: The Infinite Art of Improvisation* (Chicago, 1994) 255–56; Toni Morrison, *Beloved* (New York, 1987), 261.

1

THE DECOLONIZING VISION:
The Bluest Eye

Crumbling is not an instant's Act
A fundamental pause
Dilapidation's processes
Are organized Decays.
> —Emily Dickinson, #997

We became what we saw of ourselves in the eyes of others.
> —V. S. Naipaul, *The Mimic Men*

We only become what we are by the radical and deep-seated
refusal of that which others have made of us.
> —Jean-Paul Sartre, preface to
> Franz Fanon's *The Wretched of the Earth*

In *The Bluest Eye*, a lyricism of language channels the rage and pain of multiple privations, collusions, and exclusions into a powerful cultural critique. Recalling the pre–civil rights days of her own childhood, Toni Morrison noted that in her first novel, she saw herself as "bearing witness" to that difficult past so quickly receding in public consciousness: "It wasn't that easy. . . . Some people got slaughtered." Morrison's first novel initiates a theme that is taken up with variations in all her subsequent novels and is expressly stated in the fifth novel, *Beloved*, by Sethe, the ex-slavemother who escapes slavery: "Freeing yourself was one thing, claiming ownership of that freed self was another." Claudia MacTeer, the narrator of *The Bluest Eye* who recalls her own childhood, struggles to claim ownership of her freed self. Her struggle highlights the compromises others have made in the act of self-preservation. The novel questions these compromises, labeling them "adjustments without improvement." The profound value of this novel lies in its demystification of hegemonic social processes—in its keen grasp of the way power works, the way individuals collude in their own oppression by internalizing a dominant culture's values in the face of great material contradictions. We learn, in Terry Eagleton's words, that "emancipation thus involves that most difficult of all forms of liberation, freeing ourselves from ourselves." The novel lays bare the processes of subjectification—of identities formed through mimicry of dominant models inimical to the characters' interests, origins, and cultures. These misidentifications have a long history in slavery and in the colonization of black people, a history to which the novel makes explicit allusions; in creating these connections, the novel offers an impassioned case for decolonizing the mind.[1]

Published at the end of a decade of black cultural nationalism, *The Bluest Eye* makes clear the necessity of raising the politicized slogan *Black is beautiful* in opposition to the white monopoly on value. Yet the novel allows us to see that a mere reversing of terms (from the *ugliness* to the *beauty* of blackness) is not enough, for such counter-rhetoric does not touch the heart of the matter: the race-based class structure upheld by dominant norms and stereotypes. The novel's searing critique of domination in its various forms and its confrontation of the racially assigned class positions in the United States make it a troubling reading experience. Diane Johnson's response to Morrison's novels is a case in point. According to her, the novels leave the white reader unsure whether to accept at face value Morrison's presentation of the bizarre and shocking or to consider it symbolically; since the novels are about black people ("the oppressor in the next room") who victimize each other, they only confirm her white audience's fears about blacks.[2] Not surprisingly, while feminist critics have readily taken up *Sula*, there are fewer studies of *The Bluest Eye*; the sympathetic portrayal of the oppression of Cholly Breedlove, the poor black male who rapes his daughter, certainly complicates matters. In other words, the novel resists analysis of gender oppression that does not take into account the simultaneous impact of class and race on both men and women.

---

1. Toni Morrison, qtd. in *Identifiable Qualities*, an interview with Margaret Busby in a film by Sindamani Bridglal (England, 1989); Morrison, *Beloved*, 95; Morrison, *The Bluest Eye*, (New York, 1970); Terry Eagleton, *Ideology: An Introduction* (New York, 1991), xiii. Subsequent page references to *The Bluest Eye* will be cited within parentheses in the text.

2. Diane Johnson levels a similar charge against the novels of Gayl Jones in "The Oppressor in The Next Room," *New York Review of Books*, November 10, 1977, p. 6ff.

A remarkable feature of the novel is the foregrounding of its textual identity as the contradiction of dominant culture. The Dick-and-Jane preface and the prologue to *The Bluest Eye* establish what is certainly the hallmark of Morrison's writing, which in her own words is "the ability to be both print and oral literature," that is, to combine the layered quality of metaphoric writing (Roland Barthes's "writerly text") with the direct appeal of the narrating voice that engages the reader as listener (a "speakerly text").[3] Through its preface the novel marks its own entry as a writerly text into the print literature of a dominant culture. The arrangement of the three typographically distinct versions of the primer is a trope on writing itself. A richly suggestive metaphor that illustrates and encapsulates the primary thematic conflict in the novel, it also represents literature as the contested ground of representation, since the three versions suggest the conflictual, revisioning field of intertextuality.

The introductory *inscription* of competing texts is followed by the *voice* of the narrator juxtaposing one unnatural event of 1941—"there were no marigolds"—with another aberrant event—"Pecola was having her father's baby"—establishing Pecola as the marigold nipped in the bud (9). From the cultural images of the Dick-and-Jane text, we are led to consider the natural images of seed, flower, and earth. Both are nursery metaphors involving inculcation and cultivation. This move toward a critique of culture is central to *The Bluest Eye*. A "tragedy of cultural mutilation," *The Bluest Eye* is also the portrait of a black woman artist as a young girl breaking through sanctioned ignorance and arriving, through internal struggle, at an emergent consciousness.[4] If the third-person narratives portray the theme of subjection charting "dilapidation's processes," Claudia's first-person narrative lets us see the possibilities of an individual, and perhaps collective, resistance. This is a novel in which the community (both within the novel and outside it—the community of readers) is meant to register the burden of Pecola's tragedy. Further, even as the novel implicates its black characters in Pecola's self-abjection, its formal structure makes the reader see them all as an extended black family caught in and debilitated by a "master" narrative. Morrison achieves this unity by structuring the novel in the (dis)ordering Dick-and-Jane primer, whose model family is offered as a prototype of dominant national identity. If the primer represents

---

3. Morrison, "Rootedness," 341.

4. Barbara Christian, *Black Women Novelists: The Development of a Tradition, 1892–1976* (Westport, Conn., 1980), 149.

the classic *Bildungs* theme—the progressive acquisition of a normative, sanctioned identity—*The Bluest Eye* is an anti-*Bildungsroman* whose project is to dismantle the hegemonic norm of identity acquired through mimicry.

The Bluest Eye is an artful novel whose use of mimicry as a structuring design and a thematic concern serves to interrogate the very model being mimicked, the model that claims to be original. By confronting the negative and partial identities created by mimicry—in which only the norm (the original) can be positive or whole—the novel opens up a space for the exploration of self conceived as different from the norm, since trying to be the same as the norm is not only self-defeating (witness Pecola), but also conservative in its perpetuation of inequity.

The novel opens with a visually disorienting representation of mimicry, with three inscriptions of the Dick-and-Jane text, one "original" and two copies; the Dick-and-Jane primer is replicated with increasing typographical distortion, so that the third (and last) text is practically illegible:

Here is the house. It is green and white. It has a red door. It is very pretty. . . .

Here is the house it is green and white it has a red door it is very pretty. . . .

Hereisthehouseitisgreenandwhiteithasareddooritisverypretty

The double-spaced first text, with its capitalized sentence beginnings and standard punctuation, may be read as the "type" of self-formation that is normative in the dominant middle-class white culture. The second text, single-spaced, without the privileging signs of capital letters and the meaningful marks of punctuation, reproduces the first text with a difference that is "almost the same, but not quite." The third text reproduces the word order of the first without the benefit of spaces and stop gaps; more different from the first than the second, it is still caught in what French feminist Luce Irigaray calls "the economy of the Same."[5] Here, in brief, is an allegory of class formations and of the first world's authorizing of third world identities. The novel's strategy is to reveal the historic inequity by which the first text assumes its mastery over the third. Further, if the first text/world has set itself as the norm against which the third

5. Homi Bhabha, "Of Mimicry and Man: The Ambivalence of Colonial Discourse," *October*, XXVIII (1984), 126–27; Luce Irigaray, *This Sex Which Is Not One* (Ithaca, N.Y., 1985), 74.

is judged, the latter must always remain categorized as underdeveloped, caught in the first's definition of pathology.

Formally, the method by which the singular, primary Dick-and-Jane text organizes multiple, heterogenous identities attests to the homogenizing force of an ideology (the supremacy of "the bluest eye") by which a dominant culture reproduces hierarchical power structures. Morrison weaves a black story corresponding to each motif in the Dick-and-Jane text, so that Dick and Jane's house corresponds to the Breedloves' poor, storefront house and the Breedlove family of Pauline, Cholly, and their children, Sammy and Pecola, correspond to and contrast Mother, Father, Dick, and Jane. Ironically, in place of the pet cat and dog are two black middle-class characters, Geraldine, who loves her cat to excess, and the West Indian pedophile, Soaphead Church (as Elihue Michah Whitcomb was called by blacks in Lorain, Ohio), who hates his dog to excess. That black subjects consent to this reproduction, which leads to psychic violence among them, is also evident from the unintelligible third text. In the preface, Claudia as narrator implies that she cannot determine why the marigolds did not bloom—"since *why* is difficult to handle"—but it is clear that doing so is central to the representation of her truth. The entire novel explores the forces that lead to Pecola's desire for blue eyes. Although Morrison does not use the term hegemony, the novel illustrates a hegemonic situation. As Chandra Mukerji and Michael Schudson point out, "The question to which 'hegemony' is an answer is, 'Why do dominated or oppressed groups accept their position in the social hierarchy?' Gramsci held that oppressed groups accept the definition of the world of elites as common sense; their understanding of how the world works, then, leads them to collaborate in their own oppression."[6]

The characters' ignorance of the partisan and constructed nature of social reality leads to a consciousness turned against itself rather than the social structure. In the case of most of the characters, this "ignorance" is "smoothly cultivated," and "self-hatred" is "exquisitely learned" (55). Morrison's thematic and structural use of the Dick-and-Jane primer calls on the various meanings of *primer*. There is the obvious definition, "an elementary book for teaching children to read." But the derivation of the term cannot be ignored. A primer is a "person or thing that primes," the verb *to prime* being defined as follows:

6. Chandra Mukerji and Michael Schudson, Introduction to *Rethinking Popular Culture: Contemporary Perspectives in Cultural Studies*, ed. Mukerji and Schudson (Berkeley, 1991), 15.

"to prepare or make ready for a particular purpose or operation"; "to cover (a surface) with a preparatory coat or color, as in painting."[7] The reader is meant to see the debilitating effect of priming on the characters in the novel. There are repeated references to the various characters' miseducation, such as the following passage from Soaphead's letter to God: "We in this colony took as our own the most dramatic, and the most obvious, of our white masters' characteristics, which were, of course, their worst. In retaining the identity of our race, we held fast to those characteristics most gratifying to sustain and least troublesome to maintain. Consequently we were not royal but snobbish, not aristocratic but class-conscious, we believed authority was cruelty to our inferiors, and education was being at school" (140). This passage is similar in tone to Claudia's admission at the novel's end: "We courted death in order to call ourselves brave, and hid like thieves from life. We substituted good grammar for intellect; we switched habits to simulate maturity; we rearranged lies and called it truth, seeing in the new pattern of an old idea the Revelation and the Word"(159). Likewise, in the third-person account of the petit-bourgeois Geraldine, the narrator situates her among the "sugar-brown" southern girls whose education in respectability makes them wary of their own black "funk": "They go to land-grant colleges, normal schools, and learn how to do the white man's work with refinement: home economics to prepare his food; teacher education to instruct black children in obedience; music to soothe the weary master and entertain his blunted soul. Here they learn the rest of the lesson begun in those soft houses with porch swings and pots of bleeding heart: how to behave"(68). The project of the novel is to disrupt the educative process by which cognitive, aesthetic, and ethical values specific to the formation and interests of a socioeconomic class or group are universalized.

The difference between the second text's mimicking the first and the third text's mimicking the first are apparent in the different material situations of Geraldine and Pauline. What they have in common is an aspiration to the norm—the social, cultural, and material privileges of the first text. Because privileged class status in America has been historically coded in white terms, the accession of black people to that status is predicated on a disavowal of their race. Whatever the rhetoric of a pluralistic, democratic society, the pressure to assimilate is real. Thus, Geraldine's achievement of class security and respectability is accompanied by the repression of black "funk." This repression is

7. *Webster's New Universal Dictionary*, 1,537.

reflected typographically in the second text. In the third text, there is nothing but irony—the gross distance between ideal and reality. Pauline's attempts to be Jean Harlow only alienate her further from her own home and family.

In "The Power of Discourse and the Subordination of the Feminine," Irigaray notes that "the feminine is always described in terms of deficiency or atrophy, as the other side of the sex that alone holds a monopoly on value: the male sex." The "feminine," denied any "specificity" of its own, "provides male sexuality with an unfailingly phallic self-representation."[8] In other words, she is supposed to mimic the role of the feminine in order to shore up a masculine identity that does not recognize female difference. The above discussion of Geraldine and Pauline's mimicry of the white norm of femininity only goes to complicate Irigaray's formulation of mimicry based on the single axis of gender. Female mimicry in *The Bluest Eye* has to do with the construction of a gendered *and* racialized class hierarchy. If Irigaray's feminine subject (a universal feminine subject) is defined as lack, as absence, then the black woman is doubly lacking, for she must simulate or feign her femininity as she dissimulates or conceals her blackness. As Pecola demonstrates, this socially mandated charade of being something one is not (middle-class white girl) and of not being something one is (working-class black girl) makes one invisible, while the split mentality it entails approaches insanity.

While readers have commented on the novel's critique of consumer capitalism, the wider connections that the text makes between capitalism and colonialism, between a hegemonic institution of education and colonization, have not received critical notice.[9] Surprisingly, in the majority of criticism, Soaphead Church, the character who enables such a connection, has been glossed over. The presence of Soaphead Church implicates the mimicry of Geraldine, Pauline, and Pecola as part of colonial oppression. Homi Bhabha has situated mimicry in the context of the colonizer's project of disregarding the "cultural, racial, historical difference" of the other while securing value and priority for its own culture and race history. Education was instituted in the

8. Irigaray, *This Sex Which Is Not One*, 69–70. Because her terms are masculine and feminine, undifferentiated and uncomplicated by reference to race, we do not get the acknowledgment that in relation to the black woman, the white feminine subject is endowed with presence, priority, and wholeness.

9. Thomas H. Fick, "Toni Morrison's 'Allegory of the Cave': Movies, Consumption, and Platonic Realism in *The Bluest Eye*," *Journal of the Midwest Modern Language Association*, XX (1989), 10–22.

colonies to produce a native elite whose interests would coincide with those of the colonizers. Soaphead Church is an example of such production. In the novel, he is much more than a mere function of plot, more than an agent who will grant Pecola her blue eyes and who will substitute as the dog in the Dick-and-Jane primer. We are told that "his personality was an arabesque: intricate, symmetrical, balanced, and tightly constructed" (131), the very words we might use to describe the novel's narrative structure. His story, the last of the novel's studies in alienated consciousness, places the other accounts into perspective, for he brings from the West Indies an anglophilia and a consciousness both informed and deformed by a history of colonization. The connection between colonialism and the economic institution of the American South—domestic colonialism—was often made during the 1960s by radical analysts of black history. In the words of social critic Harold Cruse, "The only factor which differentiates the Negro's status from that of a pure colonial status is that his position is maintained in the 'home' country in close proximity to the dominant racial group."[10] The novel suggests a similarity of predicament between a colonized West Indian black subject and an African American one; both are inheritors of complex social/historical formations that vex their identities. However, the difference between Soaphead and Cholly replicates the difference between the second and third texts. Soaphead is the educated colonial gentleman who has internalized the alleged superiority of the colonizer—of his great-grandsire, the Englishman who whitened the race. Cholly is the poor, uneducated black American male doomed to the underclass who thus remains outside the hegemonic apparatus of education and class privilege. Soaphead Church's counterpart, then, is not Cholly Breedlove. A man of breeding, of metropolitan learning, the "lightly browned" Soaphead has much more in common with the "sugar brown" Geraldine. Soaphead's and Geraldine's common identity formations relate the colonies abroad and at home.

Soaphead Church, "a cinnamon-eyed West Indian," is a descendant of the Enlightenment: "A Sir Whitcomb, some decaying British nobleman, who chose to disintegrate under a sun more easeful than England's, had introduced the white strain into the family in the early 1800's" (132). We are told that the ancestral Sir Whitcomb, Jr., had a mulatta wife who, "like a good Victorian parody, learned from her husband all that was worth learning—to separate

---

10. Bhabha, "Of Mimicry and Man," 129; Gauri Viswanathan, *Masks of Conquest: Literary Study and British Rule in India* (New York, 1990); Cruse, *Rebellion or Revolution?*, 76–87.

herself in body, mind, and spirit from all that suggested Africa . . ." (132). Elihue's father, a schoolmaster, took on the white man's burden by schooling his son in "theories of education, discipline, and the good life" (133). The effect of "his father's controlled violence" was that Soaphead "develop[ed] . . . a hatred of, and fascination with, any hint of disorder and decay" (134): "He abhorred flesh on flesh. Body odor, breath odor, overwhelmed him. The sight of dried matter in the corner of the eye, decayed or missing teeth, earwax, blackheads, moles, blisters, skin crusts—all the natural excretions and protections the body was capable of—disquieted him. His attentions therefore gradually settled on those humans whose bodies were least offensive—children" (131). In Elihue Micah Whitcomb's alienation from his body, home, and nation, we are meant to see the epistemic violence and displacement wrought by the colonial project.[11]

Morrison's characterization of Soaphead invokes another West Indian protagonist, Ralph Ranjit Kripalsingh, the narrator of V. S. Naipaul's *The Mimic Men*.[12] Their similarity is worth discussing because Ralph Ranjit Kripalsingh is a loaded symbol of the kind of mimicry Morrison describes. Living in hotels and boarding houses—places that suggest profound displacement—both characters' dis-ease is acquired in part by colonial education, which has rendered them homeless. Naipaul's character is a failed politician of East Indian origin who has to leave his island in the West Indies and resign himself to "the final emptiness" of London, to "the lower-middle-class surroundings" of its suburbs. Soaphead, too, has failed to enter the ministry—that of the church—and finds himself in the United States sinking into a "rapidly fraying gentility" (135). Like Ranjit Kripalsingh, who added the name *Ralph* in order to compensate for his inadequacy, Soaphead "added the Micah" (142). Kripalsingh's name suggests a crippled being; his "book-shaped room" implicates his education as the source of his entrapment. Likewise, Soaphead's mind is described as a "soundless cave" lacking life (134). Their learning has created in them a mind-body split, leading to fastidious sexuality. Kripalsingh confesses, "Intimacy: the word holds the horror. I could have stayed for ever at a woman's breasts, if they were full and had a hint of a weight that required support. But there was the smell of

11. The term *epistemic violence* is Gayatri Spivak's from her essay "The Rani of Sirmur." The term alludes to the Western European colonial production of knowledge that justified and consolidated colonial domination while creating and subjecting its "other" via that knowledge.

12. V. S. Naipaul, *The Mimic Men* (London, 1967), 8, 25.

skin. There were bumps and scratches, there were a dozen little things that could positively enrage me." A student in London, Kripalsingh goes on to describe his "boarding house character," one similar to that of Soaphead, who has neither a flock nor a home of his own: "I took to retaining trophies from the girls who came to the book-shaped room: stockings, various small garments, once even a pair of shoes. . . ." These trophies are the flotsam of his "shipwreck." Soaphead has his own fetish collection, including "a powder blue grosgrain ribbon from the head of a little girl named Precious Jewel," and "four large hairpins." Ironically, despite Soaphead's allegiance to the great works of the masters—he has read his Shakespeare, Gibbon, and Dante—he occupies the place of the trained dog in the Dick-and-Jane text. Servile to white supremacist values, he finds it perfectly understandable that Pecola should want blue eyes and he feels gratified at being able to "grant" them to her. His biting letter to God shows him bound to the master's imperial power; after all, his nationalist rhetoric notwithstanding, it is a small piece of this power he desires, not revolution.

Like Soaphead, Geraldine has been thoroughly schooled. Hers was a train-ing in femininity and docility that would open to her the serving professions useful to the white society she wishes to enter. Educated in "normal schools," she learns "the careful development of thrift, patience, high morals, and good manners" (68). But this virtuous stability is built upon the repression of her embodied blackness, on the "get[ting] rid of the funkiness": "Wherever it erupts, this Funk, they wipe it away; where it crusts, they dissolve it; wherever it drips, flowers, or clings, they fight it until it dies. They fight this battle all the way to the grave. The laugh that is a little too loud; the enunciation a little too round; the gesture a little too generous" (68). Her distaste for the physical parallels Soaphead's. "Funk," associated with blackness and sexuality, gives her away and threatens her middle-class composure. In the slave South, the construct of purity and femininity that circumscribed white womanhood went hand-in-hand with the formulation of the black female slave as the promiscuous and lascivious other. The pervasiveness of this stereotype makes Geraldine fastid-ious and vigilant of her own sexuality. She represses "the funkiness of nature" in conformity with a bourgeois economy founded on the exclusion of color. Geraldine's distancing herself from her sexuality and race performs a conser-vative function: "do[ing] the white man's work with refinement" (68). As Michele Barrett points out, "the work of reproducing gender ideology" is facil-itated because of "women's willing consent and their internalization of oppression."[13] Geraldine is rewarded for her complicity with a certain class respectability—a green and gold house with gilded furnishings and a place in society—albeit one that mirrors the position of the pet cat who "will not play" with Jane (Pecola) in the Dick-and-Jane primer.

There is greater irony and pathos in Pauline Breedlove's desperate attempts to approximate the white middle-class norm of beauty, distanced from it as she is by her class and race. If the cultural production of gender is "to make the woman connive in treating herself as, first and foremost, a sight," the cultural production of race makes the black woman unsightly. Morrison makes it clear that while the Breedloves' poverty was "stultifying, it was not unique" (34). What is unique is their *conviction* of their ugliness, which is not an essence but a political construct supporting slavery in the past and the status quo in the present: "It was as though some mysterious all-knowing master had given each one a cloak of ugliness to wear, and they had accepted it without question. The master had said, 'you are ugly people.' They had looked about themselves and saw nothing to contradict the statement; saw, in fact, support for it leaning at them from every billboard, every movie, every glance. 'Yes,' they had said. 'You are right.' And they took their ugliness in their hands, threw it as a mantle over them, and went about the world with it" (34). The above passage corroborates W. E. B. Du Bois' 1903 statement about "this American world,—a world which yields [the black man] no true self-consciousness, but only lets him see himself through the revelation of the other world." In having Pecola seek blue eyes and ask her split self to "Please help me look" (157), Morrison shockingly dramatizes Du Bois' concept of "double consciousness," described as "this sense of always looking at one's self through the eyes of others."[14]

In fact, if culture is defined as a particular way of seeing things, then circulating images of the white male ideal of femininity—Shirley Temple on cups, Mary Jane on candy wrappers, and Jean Harlow on the screen—becomes a way of ensuring that the cultural gaze is white and male.[15] Witness Pecola,

13. See Patricia Hill Collins' essay "Mammies, Matriarchs, and Other Controlling Images," in *Black Feminist Thought: Knowledge, Consciousness, and the Politics of Empowerment* (Boston, 1990), 67–90; Michele Barrett, "Ideology and the Cultural Production of Gender," in *Feminist Criticism and Social Change*, ed. Judith Newton and Deborah Rosenfelt (New York, 1985), 80–81.

14. John Berger, *Ways of Seeing* (Harmondsworth, Eng., 1972), 51; W. E. B. Du Bois, *The Souls of Black Folk* (New York, 1969), 45.

15. Arif Dirlik, "Culturalism as Hegemonic Ideology and Liberating Practice," *Cultural Critique*, VI (Spring, 1987), 13.

who has "nine lovely orgasms with three Mary Janes" from the candy whose wrapper has the picture of the blond-haired, blue-eyed girl: "To eat the candy is somehow to eat the eyes, eat Mary Jane. Love Mary Jane. Be Mary Jane" (43). The ubiquitous self-representation of the white subject as the universal subject reinscribes the other as lack. This is dramatized in the episode of Pauline turning herself into a "sight." The locus of this mimicry is, aptly enough, a cinema theatre; sitting with her hair styled after Jean Harlow's while looking at the movie star from the vantage of the white male gaze, Pauline erases her own identity. This abject loss of self is depicted in her fallen tooth, loosened while eating Mary Jane candy and watching Jean Harlow. So much for romantic love and beauty.

It is Claudia's narrative that grounds this ideology of beauty/ugliness in the concrete material relations it sustains. She tells us that in the vicinity of the railroad tracks—the section of town where her family lives—the sky burns "with a dull orange glow"; they can "see the great carloads of slag being dumped, red hot and smoking, into the ravine that skirts the steel mill" (12). In marked contrast, while walking to the lake-front Fisher house, where Pauline Breedlove works as a maid, Claudia notes that the "orange-patched sky of the steel-mill section never reached this part of town. The sky was always blue" (84). On reaching "the large white house with the wheelbarrow full of flowers," she "circle[s] the proud house" and goes "to the back" in search of Pecola: "There on the tiny railed stoop sat Pecola in a light red sweater and blue cotton dress. A little wagon was parked near her" (84). In contrast to "the wheelbarrow full of flowers," the wagon beside Pecola is soon going to be "heavy with wet clothes," the Fishers' laundry (87). The pretty white house is literally backed by black Pecola just as the lakeside beauty and wealth of this industrial town is backed by the smoking steel plant in which a worker like Cholly Breedlove must "adjust to . . . cutbacks" (34). In accepting the stigmatized identity that her race confers on her, Pauline Breedlove ends up negating her daughter while maintaining a social order (the white Fisher household) that recognizes her only as "the ideal servant" (101).

While Soaphead and Geraldine fight signs of corporeal decay, Pauline and Cholly Breedlove fight each other. They steadily decay spiritually, their inner state manifested by rotting teeth—literal rot for Pauline, metaphorical for Cholly. If Pauline's lost tooth attests to her failure to be what she mimics, Cholly's pulled tooth symbolizes his emasculation (119). He is represented as outside or beyond the norm. Unfathered, unsocialized, and "castrated" early in his youth by an encounter with white men—recall how hunters with flashlights made a spectacle of his love-making with a black girl, Darlene—he is a social derelict, as much outside the system of race, class, and gender privilege as Pecola. This makes him, ironically, a free man, a descendant of the freedmen who, after slavery was abolished, were expected to divest themselves of the trauma of having been slave breeders—denied the opportunity to father their offspring and fit themselves into monogamous units called families. This impossibility, the narrator tells us, was the "pervading ache of freedom" that black musicians made songs of: "The pieces of Cholly's life become coherent only in the head of a musician. . . . Only a musician would sense, know, without even knowing that he knew, that Cholly was free. Dangerously free" (125).

From Cholly's point of view, that of the radical outsider, monogamy is "a curious and an unnatural idea" (126) and the family an institution based upon "the accumulation of things" requiring "material heirs" (127). Although depicted as the inverse of the "big and strong" and "smiling" Father of the Dick-and-Jane text, he enters Pauline's life in a "godlike state" (126) : "He came, strutting right out of a Kentucky sun on the hottest day of the year. He came big, he came strong, he came with yellow eyes, flaring nostrils, and he came with his own music" (91). However, his helplessness arises after his marriage in relation to the normal masculine roles of husband, father, and breadwinner. His failure to provide for his family is implicated in a larger historic contradiction in which an economically and politically emasculated man is expected to simulate the power and stability of masculinity. As Francis Beale observes, "unfortunately, neither the Black man nor the Black woman understood the true nature of the forces working upon them. Many Black women tended to accept the capitalist evaluation of manhood and womanhood and believed, in fact, that Black men were shiftless and lazy, otherwise they would get a job and support their families as they ought to. Personal relationships between Black men and women were thus torn asunder and one result has been the separation of man from wife, mother from child, etc."[16] The historic powerlessness in relation to the white male power structure translates into power in relation to the poor black girl/woman. Cholly's actual rape of Pecola is echoed by Soaphead's metaphoric one. The lines describing Soaphead's encounter with Pecola could easily belong to the section describing Cholly's rape of her: "A surge of

16. Francis Beale, "Double Jeopardy," in The Black Woman, ed. Toni Cade (New York, 1970), 90.

love and understanding swept through him [Soaphead], but was quickly replaced by anger. Anger that he was powerless to help her. . . . His outrage grew
and felt like power" (137).

Morrison's account of the conditions under which Pecola was born and made
invisible could be read in the context of Ralph Ellison's preoccupation with
the invisibility of the black man and Richard Wright's indifference to the
muting of the black woman. As Michael Awkward notes, "Morrison writes her
way into the Afro-American literary tradition by foregrounding the effects of
incest for female victims in direct response to Ellison's refusal to consider them
seriously." We may also recall Richard Wright's exclusive concern in *Native
Son* with "how Bigger was born" and his apparent disregard of how his girlfriend
Bessie was killed (by Bigger); in fact, the narrator makes no apology for this
neglect: "The loud demand of the tensity of his own body was a voice that
drowned out hers."[17] Morrison supplements Wright's perspective of the subaltern black man with a feminist one. But if Wright drowns out Bessie's voice,
readers may well wonder if Morrison denies Pecola her voice; after all, the
effect of silencing is similar: "The gigantic thrust he made into her then pro-
voked the only sound she made—a hollow suck of air in the back of her throat"
(128).

While Morrison lifts Pecola out of her invisibility, she also covers for Cholly
Breedlove as Ellison does for Trueblood, as Wright does for Bigger Thomas.
Even as the text indicates the oppressive part the black male plays in consigning
the poor black girl/woman to her role as the "mule of the world"—Zora Neale
Hurston's phrase—Morrison is careful to prevent a reading in which Pecola's
father is the villain. At the outset, a series of parallel statements turning from
the literal to the figural place Cholly in the same category as the MacTeer
sisters:"*We had dropped our seeds in our own little plot of black dirt just as Pecola's
father had dropped his seeds in his own plot of black dirt. Our innocence and faith
were no more productive than his lust or despair. What is clear now is that of all that
hope, fear, lust, love, and grief, nothing remains but Pecola and the unyielding earth.
Cholly Breedlove is dead; our innocence too. The seeds shrivelled and died; her baby
too*" (9). The prologue forewarns against a metaleptic reading that takes the
effects as causes; only nine-year-olds may be excused for thinking "that it was

17. Michael Awkward, *Inspiriting Influences: Tradition, Revision, and Afro-American Women's
Novels* (New York, 1989), 87; Richard Wright, *Native Son* (New York, 1987), 219.

because Pecola was having her father's baby that the marigolds did not grow" (9).

Beginning with an admission of the narrator's childhood guilt—"For years I thought . . . it was my fault. I had planted them [marigold seeds] too far down in the earth" (9)—the novel ends with the narrator broadening the *I* to *we*, clearly implicating members of a certain "well behaved," "licensed" class: "All of us—all who knew her—felt so wholesome after we cleaned ourselves on her. We were so beautiful when we stood astride her ugliness. . . . Her poverty kept us generous" (159). Here Morrison is clearly aligning her feminist concern with a critique of the black middle class, so that Cholly, by virtue of not belonging to this class, escapes frontal blame for his abuse of Pecola and the educated Soaphead Church receives more contempt for his metaphoric rape of her. The novel, addressing the educated *we* of the emergent black nationalists, lays its own feminist claim to represent the subaltern, for whom the nationalist movement came "much, much too late" (160).

The Bluest Eye is considered by most readers to be a rather bleak novel, for the events it plots evince little hope. However, through Claudia's growing understanding of the meaning of Pecola's story, Morrison is staging an emergent consciousness. A narrative about Pecola Breedlove's subjection, *The Bluest Eye* is also a portrait of the artist as a black girl who "considered all speech a code to be broken . . . all gestures subject to careful analysis" (149). Claudia MacTeer's narrative of childhood is impelled by a desire to relive and reflect upon the personal and the past in order to comprehend its lived exclusions. Through Claudia's first-person account, the consciousness of childhood is given an adult understanding, the utopian energy of uninhibited desire channeled toward a political critique. In order to move beyond the closed story of complicity, victimization, and subjection, in order to speak of change and resistance, the novel has to rely on characters at the margins of the normalizing forces plotted by the text: on Claudia as a yet-to-be-normalized child who is both inside and outside the narrative of subjection, and on the three whores who are outside the dominant and dominating narrative of middle-class norms.

As Carolyn Kay Steedman notes, in returning to events "back in the past . . . the only point lies in interpretation." "All children," she observes, "experience a first loss, a first exclusion," but it "will be differently reinterpreted by the adult who used to be the child, according to the social circumstances she finds herself in, and the story she needs to relate." Morrison's account of childhood's first loss and exclusion has to do with a sense of being a have-not, of acquiring a gender, race, and class consciousness, expressed in the feeling of envy, redefined by Steedman as the "social and subjective sense of the impossible unfairness of things." Defining working-class consciousness as "a structure of feeling" that is "learned in childhood," Steedman describes "one of its components a proper envy, the desire of people for the things of the earth." Claudia's encounter with Rosemary Villanucci, the daughter of a European immigrant sitting in her father's 1939 Buick, while eating bread and butter, speaks of the abrasiveness of thwarted desire: "She rolls down the window to tell my sister Frieda and me that we can't come in. We stare at her, wanting her bread, but more than that wanting to poke the arrogance out of her eyes and smash the pride of ownership that curls her chewing mouth. When she comes out of the car we will beat her up, make red marks on her white skin." (12). Steedman's remarks on the sociopolitical implications of articulating envy illumine Morrison's staged opening. Steedman observes that the civilized sanction against expressions of envy—itself considered a sin—represses the truth of "material and psychological deprivation" undoubtedly felt by countless marginal subjects: "by allowing this envy entry into political understanding, the proper struggles of people in a state of dispossession to gain their inheritance might be seen not as sordid and mindless greed for the things of the market place, but attempts to alter a world that has produced in them states of unfulfilled desire."[18] Such feelings are socially inadmissible because they carry the potential of a vision that would challenge that of the bluest eye.

The child's encounter with the various "prohibitions and proscriptions" of the world "can be seen as the place where a child enters a culture, and a culture comes to occupy a child." In so far as a child's consciousness is outside the world of adult norms, it is also oppositional to it. While Pecola's story depicts the inexorable process by which she is occupied by culture, Claudia's records her refusal to learn the dominant scripts of race, class, and gender. By revisiting her childhood rage against blond, blue-eyed dolls, symbolic of the disabling gender identity that her mother (in accord with the rest of society) thrust upon her, Claudia highlights her own resistance to the socialization and acculturation that cripples Pecola and other characters. In contrast to the mimic men and women in the novel, Claudia questions the impulse to mimic, accurately per-

---

18. Carolyn Kay Steedman, *Landscape For a Good Woman: A Story of Two Lives* (New Brunswick, N.J., 1987), 5–6, 116, 111, 7, 123.

ceiving it as a desire the environment persuades her to internalize: "From the clucking sound of adults I knew that the doll represented what they thought was my fondest wish. . . . Adults, older girls, shops, magazines, newspapers, window signs—all the world had agreed that a blue-eyed, yellow-haired, pink-skinned doll was what every girl child treasured" (19–20). Finding the doll undesirable, Claudia subjects it to a ruthless examination, reducing it to its material constituents of "sawdust," "gauze," "disk with six holes," and "a mere, metal roundness" (21). In the same way, Morrison explodes the unity of the Dick-and-Jane text, demystifying its claim to be imitable. It is befitting that all the sections of Claudia's heretical narrative are free of the coercive "dickand-jane" epigraphs that head the narratives of mimicry, for resistance as a praxis separate from and opposed to mimicry constitutes nothing less than a transformation in consciousness. Toni Cade, editor of *The Black Woman*, an anthology of essays published in 1970, the same year as *The Bluest Eye*, echoes Claudia's way out of alienation: "you find your Self in destroying illusions, smashing myths, laundering the head of whitewash, being responsible to some truth, to the struggle."[19]

As Raymond Williams points out, although hegemony is "a whole body of practices and expectations," in which "the whole lived social process [is] practically organized by specific and dominant meanings and values," "it is never either total or exclusive." In other words, the possibility of contestation is not precluded; there is scope for "smashing myths" and for "laundering the head," which is what the novel does. Such a contestation entails the creation of a new consciousness, what Williams calls "a specific practice of self-making," a "creative practice" that is an "active struggle." It is, in his words, "the long and difficult re-making of an inherited (determined) practical consciousness: a process often described as development but in practice a struggle at the roots of the mind—not casting off an ideology, or learning phrases about it, but confronting a hegemony in the fibres of the self and in the hard practical substance of effective and continuing relationships."[20]

Claudia MacTeer, in her successful emergence from hegemonic constraints, lives this idea of creative practice. What makes it possible for her to resist the dominant culture is the strong presence of an alternative culture at home passed on to her by her mother, whose blues songs "about trains and Arkansas" (78),

19. *Ibid.*, 111; Cade, "On the Issue of Roles," in *The Black Woman*, 108.
20. Williams, *Marxism and Literature*, 109, 113, 210–12.

spirited diatribes against Henry Ford and Franklin Delano Roosevelt, and kitchen conversations with the neighborhood black women punctuated with "warm-pulsed laughter" (16), emit the resilience of a cultural identity of resistance. That Mrs. MacTeer is also outraged by Claudia's refusal to love the blue-eyed dolls is an illustration of the power of dominant values to achieve a certain degree of consensus, to insinuate themselves "in the fibres of the self."

Besides Claudia, who unlearns her way into an enabling selfhood, the only characters in the novel who do not look at themselves through the eyes of others are the three whores, "amused by a long-ago time of ignorance" (47). According to Elliott Butler-Evans, the three whores "are almost totally unrelated to the novel's dominant focus." This statement is true only if one ignores the dual focus of the novel, which counters the abjection of mimicry by enacting the reclamation of self through acts of resistance. The whores—China, Poland, and Marie, who is also called "the Maginot Line"—serve the latter focus. Their function is to literally embody a positive, oppositional space in the novel. The body/bawdy imagery characterizing these women is radically opposed to bourgeois norms. Speaking of Paule Marshall's novels, Susan Willis makes a statement that could well apply to Morrison's fiction: "In all of Marshall's novels, the transformation out of bourgeois encumbrances and values is enacted physically on the bodies of her female characters. The body provides a medium for metaphors of history, making these metaphors experientially concrete."[21] In Morrison's fiction, negative and positive states of being in the world are always physically embodied. The individual body becomes the primary site of culture; though it is disciplined, it can also intervene, revolt, or impose its own alternative bodily knowledge and presence. Defeat of the self in Morrison's fiction is characterized by body imagery that has to do with shame, suppression, and shrinkage; the dissenting self inhabits a robust body that refuses to atomize itself or rid itself of "funk." Pecola mentally effaces her body by imagining the disappearance of her limbs. In contrast, Claudia's interest in the "neat and nasty" nature of her own puke—"green-gray, with flecks of orange," "stubbornly clinging to its own mass, refusing to break up and be removed" (13)—functions as a sign of her robust consciousness. Her aesthetics are her own, and like the glutinous particles clinging to their own mass, Claudia stubbornly resists being

---

21. Elliott Butler-Evans, *Race, Gender, and Desire: Narrative Strategies in the Fiction of Toni Cade Bambara, Toni Morrison, and Alice Walker* (Philadelphia, 1989), 79; Willis, *Specifying*, 80.

administered by others. In her loathing of "the unimaginative cleanliness" enforced by "hateful baths," her irritation with the "scratchy towels and the dreadful and humiliating absence of dirt" (21), Claudia is defending the child's delight in the body from the adult's suppression of it. Claudia rues the alienation from her own body in submitting to adult norms: "Gone the ink marks from legs and face, all my creations and accumulations of the day gone, and replaced by goose pimples" (21). As we have seen in the case of Geraldine and Soaphead Church, order and decorum is obtained at the expense of creativity and results in a body alienated from its own eros.

Like Claudia, the three whores reveal the difference between inhabiting the body and inhibiting it. They occupy space without apology. Interestingly, they are represented as the "three merry gargoyles" (47), described in the *Oxford English Dictionary* as roof spouts carved in grotesque human or animal figures "projected as gutters carrying rainwater away from the wall," in order to protect and preserve property. In the socioeconomic architecture of capitalist patriarchy, the institutions of marriage, family, and private property are conserved by prostitutes functioning as gargoyles. Morrison's whores, with their "rain-soaked eyes" and "eyes as clean as rain" (82), preserve the family structure by releasing illicit male desire. Unlike the other characters in the novel, they understand the social parameters of their position and, in their refusal to accept sentimental or normative representations of themselves, are incorruptible in their "corruption": "They did not belong to those generations of prostitutes created in novels, with great and generous hearts, dedicated . . . to ameliorating the luckless, barren life of men, taking money incidentally and humbly for their 'understanding.' Nor were they from that sensitive breed of young girl, gone wrong at the hands of fate . . . knowing full well she was cut out for better things, and could make the right man happy" (47). Since romance is oxymoronic to their commerce with men, they remain clear-eyed about their roles: "They were whores in whores' clothing" (48). Their names are suggestive of their refusal to be co-opted. In their occupations as whores, the women bear the same relationship to patriarchy that the occupied territories of China, Poland, and France (the Maginot Line bearing a synecdochic relationship to France) have to Japan and Nazi Germany in World War II. A significant fact about China, Poland, and France, as Wilfred Samuels and Clenora Hudson-Weems note, is that "these places were not annihilated and their cultural values did not crumble." Beseiged though the women are, they are not merely walls to be broken or lines to be transgressed; a triumvirate, the three whores are at war with men: "these women hated men, all men without shame, apology, or discrimination. . . . Black men, white men, Puerto Ricans, Mexicans, Jews, Poles, whatever—all were inadequate and weak, all . . . were the recipients of their disinterested wrath" (47).

Officially marginalized and condemned by the social order they help support, the three merry gargoyles are aware of their important function. Singers of blues songs, concocters of lewd stories that are "breezy and rough," alluding to sex and the joys of finger-licking food, these women laugh, drink, belch, and swear. Their aesthetics and ethics are radically different from those of the dominant culture—and the black middle class—centered on property and propriety. They are the only source of laughter in this sombre novel: "All three of the women laughed. Marie threw back her head. From deep inside, her laughter came like the sound of many rivers, freely, deeply, muddily, heading for the room of an open sea. China giggled spastically. . . . Poland . . . laughed without sound" (45). In fact, Morrison's characterization of them bears a striking affinity to the imagery of the grotesque that Bakhtin outlines in relation to the "folk carnival humor" he found in Rabelais's work. Infused with "the sense of the gay relativity of prevailing truths and authorities"—what Bakhtin calls *carnivalesque*—the following parley between China and Marie flouts bourgeois decorum.[22]

"How come you always say 'Whoa Jesus' and a number?" . . .

"Because my mama taught me never to cuss."

"Did she teach you not to drop your drawers?" China asked.

"Didn't have none," said Marie. "Never saw a pair of drawers till I was fifteen, when I left Jackson and was doing day work in Cincinnati. My white lady gave me some old ones of hers. I thought they was some kind of stocking cap. I put it on my head when I dusted. When she saw me, she liked to fell out."

"You must have been one dumb somebody." China lit a cigarette and cooled her irons.

"How'd I know?" Marie paused. "And what's the use of putting on something you got to keep taking off all the time?" (46)

The satiric repartee reveals that Marie knows what Pauline Breedlove in her Jean Harlow hairdo does not: that the norms of the first text do not apply to the third.

22. Wilfred D. Samuels and Clenora Hudson-Weems, *Toni Morrison* (Boston, 1990), 21; Mikhail Bakhtin, Introduction to *Rabelais and His World*, trans. Helene Iswolsky (Bloomington, Ind., 1984), 11.

Bakhtin coins the term *grotesque realism* for the aesthetic of the antibourgeois culture of carnival, with its celebration of "the material bodily principle." In this style, characterized by exaggeration, "the bodily element is deeply positive," not presented "in a private, egotistic form, severed from the other spheres of life."[23] We have seen the private version in the depiction of Geraldine; in contrast, consider the following description of the Maginot Line as she sits on the second-story porch: "A mountain of flesh, she lay rather than sat in a rocking chair . . . swollen ankles smoothed and tightened the skin; massive legs like tree stumps parted wide at the knees, over which spread two roads of soft flabby inner thigh that kissed each other deep in the shade of her dress and closed. A dark-brown root-beer bottle like a burned limb, grew out of her dimpled hand. She looked at us . . . and emitted a low, long belch. Her eyes were as clean as rain, and again I remembered the waterfall" (82). Portrayed in epic dimensions, the Maginot Line's body is organically powerful (mountain, waterfall, tree stump). In her massive force—one not easily overcome—she counters the genteel image of the isolated Geraldine wiping out all expressions of funk. Refusing the Maginot Line's smiling offer to the MacTeer sisters to come up and have some pop, Frieda baldly explains that they are forbidden to enter her house: "My mama said you ruined." Marie retaliates with the carnivalesque weapon of laughter: "The waterfalls began to run again. . . . The Maginot Line put a fat hand on one of the folds of her stomach and laughed. At first just a deep humming with her mouth closed, then a larger, warmer sound. Laughter at once beautiful and frightening. She let her head tilt sideways, closed her eyes, and shook her massive trunk, letting the laughter fall like a wash of red leaves all around us. Scraps and curls of the laughter followed us as we ran" (83). Not simply an obedient conduit of male desire, this social gargoyle counters the offensive hypocrisy of respectability with the "deep humming" sound of derisive artillery.

Through the portrayals of Pauline Breedlove and the three whores, the novel registers its deep sympathy with the predicament of rural, working-class black folk in the industrial North and their ensuing inscription—whether consenting or dissenting—into the celluloid dreams of romantic love and physical beauty predicated on white middle-class values. Born and educated in the North, Claudia MacTeer is caught between two worlds: the working-class world of the Breedloves and the educated middle-class world of Geraldine. The

23. Bakhtin, *Rabelais and His World*, 18–19.

resolution of her conflict lies in explaining or advocating the interests and desires of the former to the latter—in doing so, she reveals the middle-class identity as a product of mobility achieved by its difference from, and indifference to, the working class. Claudia's concern is one that underwrites all of Toni Morrison's work.

In her next novel, *Sula*, Morrison explores from the viewpoint of black female adolescence and adulthood what in *The Bluest Eye* she recollects from the viewpoint of black female childhood: lives lived amidst social and economic limitations. Claudia's spirit of rebellion is resurrected in Sula, whose pride and reckless breaking of norms oppressive to black women takes her beyond the protection of her community, which, like the one in *The Bluest Eye*, is ridden with prejudices—those of the dominant group and those it has developed in trying to cope with domination.

2

FREEDOM'S ABSENT HORIZON:
Sula

I used to live in this world . . . I used to really belong here.
And at some point I didn't belong here anymore. I was
somebody's parent, somebody's this, somebody's that, but there
was no me in this world. And I was looking for that dead girl
and I thought I might talk about that dead girl . . . not only
was that girl dead in my mind, I thought she was dead in
everybody's mind. . . . I didn't know what happened. I had
been living some other person's life. And then I got to
thinking about this girl, this woman. If it wasn't conventional,
she didn't want it. She was willing to risk in her imagination a
lot of things and pay the price and also go astray.
              —Toni Morrison, "A Conversation:
                  Gloria Naylor and Toni Morrison"

. . . History may be servitude,
History may be freedom. See, now they vanish,
The faces and places, with the self which, as it could,
      loved them,
To become renewed, transfigured, in another pattern.
              —T. S. Eliot, "Little Gidding,"
                  Four Quartets

Sula begins and ends by mourning the past displaced and forgotten by the
post-1965 integrationist era. The reader is informed from the beginning that
the narrative itself is a commemorative act for an extinct community, "the
Bottom," now replaced by suburbs and a golf course. In its elegiac mood we
find no nationalist celebration of the victories of integration—only a registering

of cultural death. One is reminded of Yevgeny Yevtushenko's poem "People," in which the poet makes his "lament against destruction" for "the secret worlds" that "cannot be brought back": "by the rule of the game something has gone / Not people die but worlds die in them."[1] The focal point in this novel about multiple deaths is the social death of the female self.

The novel represents the history of a segregated community in Medallion, Ohio, as a protracted war, with soldiers of both genders becoming casualties: "Peace" (the title character's family name) is absent in this book of wounds and schisms, losses and injustices at the individual and collective level. The novel seethes with desire and its many social curtailments: the desire of Ajax to fly planes, the desire of Jude to do meaningful work, the desire of Sula and Nel to experience the exhilaration of self-discovery. Each of these desires is alienated. "Where human subjects politically begin, in all their sensuous specificity, is with certain needs and desires," writes Terry Eagleton. "Yet need and desire are also what render us nonidentical with ourselves, opening us up to some broader social dimension; and what is posed within this dimension is the question of what *general* conditions would be necessary for our particular needs and desires to be fulfilled." By representing the death of "inalienable" desires, the novel condemns the absence of these conditions even as it invites an envisioning of them. If the novel is a posthumous "medallion" for its wounded braves—shell-shocked veterans such as Shadrack and Plum, men with truncated aspirations such as Ajax and Jude—it is a searing requiem for the isolation, mangled creativity, and loveless lives of women such as Eva, Hannah, Sula, and Nel. The persistent ache in the novel's prose signifies "the insistent pressure of *freedom* as the *absent horizon*," a point Kumkum Sangari made regarding the narratives of Gabriel García Márquez. Freedom's horizon is "precisely that which is made present and possible by its absence—the lives that people have never lived *because* of the lives they are forced to live or have chosen to live. That which is desired and that which exists, the sense of abundance and the sense of waste, are dialectically related."[2]

Although *Sula* is structured by linear, chronological time, with each chapter

1. Yevgeny Yevtushenko, "People," *Selected Poems*, trans. Robin Milner-Guland and Peter Levi (New York, 1962), 85–86.

2. Terry Eagleton, "Nationalism, Irony and Commitment," *Nationalism, Colonialism and Literature: Terry Eagleton, Fredric Jameson, and Edward Said* (Minneapolis, Minn., 1990) 37–38; Sangari, "Politics of the Possible," 176.

headed by year, these allusive, broadly referential dates serve as public markers for the narratives of private loves and griefs. Here, as in all Morrison's novels, historic time is best understood through the duration of private lives, where personal experience in turn acquires its significance only within a historical process. An episodic narrative marked by skips and jumps in time from 1919 to 1965, the novel proceeds with flashbacks and tantalizing gaps, privileging a circular, mnemonic time. The narrator provides certain facts, but the drawing of connections is left to the reader. Commenting on the storyteller's craft, Walter Benjamin observes: "Actually, it is half the art of storytelling to keep a story free from explanation as one reproduces it. . . . The most extraordinary things, marvelous things, are related with the greatest accuracy, but the psychological connection of the events is not forced on the reader. It is left up to him to interpret things the way he understands them, and thus the narrative achieves an amplitude that information lacks."[3]

The novel's poignant and intense nature derives from the lived tensions of hierarchical structures—those of top-bottom, black-white, haves–have-nots, male-female, heterosexual marriage–female friendship. Though racialized economic discrimination wounds both men and women in this mostly segregated black community, the lives of women like Sula and Nel become a reproach to the gender roles subordinating women, roles the community enforces in the name of black solidarity and survival.

Sula chronicles the history of the Bottom through a feminist lens. Henry Louis Gates, Jr., observes that black culture "is a self-enclosed mythos, also existing apart from the social dynamism of white racism." The Bottom raises its own metaphysical defenses against the evils of racism, upholds its own self-regulating code of ethics. But if collective marginalization brings about a group's cohesiveness, it also makes the group critical of radical departures from its norms. What makes the Bottom a haven to the flotsam and jetsam of society (disabled veterans, drunken disconsolates such as Tar Baby, the homeless Deweys) is also what makes it develop into a restrictive community. Its acceptance of difference and anomaly seems to extend only to the victimized; any assertion of independence from the communal codes of conduct—especially by its women—is viewed with hostility. Such autonomy is considered an unwelcome departure by a beleaguered group whose energies are geared toward self-preservation.

3. Benjamin, *Illuminations*, 89.

Anger at the economic structure that keeps them down is vented on an enemy within, who appears to threaten a precariously functioning world. By heaping their anger on Sula, the community channels its deep frustration within its own bounds. Where racial bonds forged in the oppressive crucible of history exert a centripetal, unifying force upon the group, Sula's assertion of female selfhood—claiming freedom from structural roles of gender—is seen as divisive, as a centrifugal force to react against (especially since it has been the black woman's historic burden to be the unifying force of a culture under siege). As Madhu Dubey notes, "*Sula* plays nationalism and feminism against each other" in "a dynamic contradiction"; the tensions between the beleaguered community and the heretic Sula are expressive of "the counterpressure exerted by black nationalist ideology on a feminist articulation of black femininity."[4] The novel enables us to see in Sula's heresy the impossible response of one seeking to exceed the socially imposed limits of the possible.

The opening chapter carefully locates the lives of Sula and Nel—and the emergent question of feminism—within the larger narrative of the community. Although Sula and her outlawed feminist desire stand out against the bottomed-out community, the community itself is shown as being *productive* of Sula's desire. A novel of catclysmic upheavals in which fire destroys, water drowns, and ice kills, *Sula* evokes death at many levels, concerned as it is with a black community's experience of life and all that kills or maims its expression. The reader witnesses both the ritualistic installation of Shadrack's National Suicide Day on January 3, 1920, and the literal enactment of it twenty years later, on January 3, 1941, a year after the death of Sula. If the emotional center of the novel is the consciousness of one young black woman (as its title indicates), then the family, community, and outer world are the spokes that intersect in the figure of Sula, so that in her defiance and complexity, she radiates their influence.

Typically in nationalist struggles, feminism has been required to remain several steps behind nationalism. R. Radhakrishnan poses a vital question of asymmetry: "Why is it that the advent of the politics of nationalism signals the subordination if not the demise of women's politics? Why does the politics of the 'one' typically overwhelm the politics of the 'other'? Why could the two

---

4. Henry Louis Gates, Jr., "Tell Me, Sir, . . . What Is 'Black' Literature?" *PMLA*, CV (1990), 20; Madhu Dubey, *Black Women Novelists and the Nationalist Aesthetic* (Bloomington, Ind., 1994), 51.

not be coordinated within an equal and dialogic relationship of mutual accountability? . . . Faced with its own repression, the women's question seems
forced either to seek its own separatist political autonomy or to envision other
ways of constituting a relational-integrative politics."[5] In representing the collective experience of alienation from a feminist consciousness, *Sula* overturns
the historic erasure of feminist concerns by the politics of nationalism. However, *Sula* does not replicate the errors of nationalism by advocating an exclusive priority of feminism over other concerns. Instead, feminism in *Sula* pow-
erfully informs collective concerns.

Sula is the iconoclastic figuration of black feminism attempting to break
through nationalist consciousness. Her early and unexplained death reveals
the absence of a viable feminist space within black collectivity. Through the
poetics of loss, the novel attempts to bridge the epistemological gap between
the disheartened desires and aspirations that go by the name of "Sula" and
those of the community. Sula's death in 1940 ostensibly should have delivered
the Bottom. But instead the community is assailed by another economic depression in a winter that chills their bones. Joining the National Suicide Day
procession in 1941, members of the community "are suddenly quiet" on reaching the tunnel they were not allowed to build: "Their hooded eyes swept over
the place where their hope had lain since 1927. There was the promise: leaf-
dead. The teeth unrepaired, the coal credit cut off, the chest pains unattended,
the school shoes unbought, the rush-stuffed mattresses, the broken toilets, the
leaning porches, the slurred remarks and the staggering childish malevolence
of their employers." The source of their misery becomes clear "in blazing sunlit
ice rapidly becoming water."[6] Sula is not the problem. More than two decades
after Sula's death, in a parallel coming-to-consciousness, Nel realizes that all
along her comrade and partner in struggle has been none other than Sula.

What Sula and the Bottom folk—who have labeled malevolence "Sula"—
have in common is a failed insurgency. The community's revolt against economic oppression—the collective, self-immolating protest at the tunnel—is
no more productive than Sula's revolt against the Bottom's gender roles. The
gap between the sundered and defeated emancipatory projects is breached in
the figure of Nel, in whose consciousness this double loss—of Sula and of the

5. Radhakrishnan, "Nationalism, Gender, and the Narrative of Identity," 78.

6. Toni Morrison, *Sula* (New York, 1973), 161. Subsequent page references will be cited
within parentheses in the text.

Bottom—is registered. The novel is able to assert the legitimacy of a black feminist position by staging a poetics of loss. Toni Morrison's comment to Gloria Naylor about the "dead girl" points to the alienation of women from themselves. If Sula is the dead girl, she also represents the female self sabotaged by the community's "good woman," Nel, who as a pubescent girl had said "me" in front of the mirror: "She got out of bed and lit the lamp to look in the mirror. . . . 'I'm me,' she whispered. 'Me.' Nel didn't know quite what she meant, but on the other hand she knew exactly what she meant. . . . Each time she said the word 'me' there was a gathering in her like power, like joy, like fear" (28). Nel's early assimilation of her self—her "me"—into her husband Jude's self, her abandoning the creative project of her own self-making for his struggle with subordination within the dominant social order, can be read as the project of a masculinist nationalism assimilating and erasing the claims of feminism: "The two of them together would make one Jude" (83). Such an assimilation is emphatically refused by Sula. However, her stance costs her dearly; she lives and dies in isolation.

In Sula's estranged friend Nel, the novel recuperates a feminist consciousness suffocated in its nascency. It also reactivates a black nationalist narrative of disenchantment with progress—"Things were so much better in 1965. Or so it seemed" (163). Freedom of self-definition remains elusive for the Bottom, itself now dispersed. Nel's concern for the community—rather, her concern over the postintegration disintegration of community—is climaxed by her belated recognition of Sula and of her alienation from herself. Nel's emergent consciousness is the breakthrough the novel offers: "'Sula?' she whispered, gazing at the tops of trees. 'Sula?' . . . And the loss pressed down on her chest and came up into her throat. . . . 'O Lord, Sula,' she cried, 'girl, girl, girlgirlgirl.' It was a fine cry—loud and long—but it had no bottom and it had no top, just circles and circles of sorrow" (174).

Nel and Sula's alienation finds its meaning in a larger social history. The novel parallels two distinct matrilineal genealogies of class and color: Eva, Hannah, and Sula Peace chart a working-class history of black women from the post-Reconstruction era, from 1895 to 1940; the light-skinned Rochelle, Helene Wright, and Nel Wright Greene represent the bourgeois ascendance from and disavowal of subaltern black origins rendered shameful and inaccessible by the bourgeois morality of domesticity and respectability. Nel is the descendant of an ancestral house in New Orleans where the presence of "four Virgin Marys" was meant to exorcise "the red shutters," "soft lights," and "gardenia smell" exemplary of Rochelle, her Creole grandmother who worked as a prostitute (25). Fearfully and aggressively, Helene Wright cultivates respectability lest the wayward morals and "wild blood" of Rochelle (her mother) betray her, disrupting her, and later Nel's, right to a brick porch house and a husband. Helene's denial of her blackness is a measure of her class aspirations in a society where economic privilege is color-coded; in her we see the success of an ideology of race that is also made visible in other light-skinned Morrison characters: Geraldine in *The Bluest Eye*, Dr. Foster and his daughter Ruth in *The Song of Solomon*. Helene's fearful gift to her daughter Nel is a clothespin, the instrument for forming her broad nose into an appropriately shaped one: "Don't you want a nice nose when you grow up?" (55). This homely instrument of torture is a symbol of the nurturing denied Nel. Although under Sula's influence she abandons the clothespin, Nel remains unable to assert herself in relation to Jude. Nel is prepared by her upbringing to perform an entirely secondary and supporting role as wife, to collaborate in her own negation, so that her love for him "over the years [spins] a steady gray web around her heart" (95).

Raised without men in a household of independent women, Sula grows up as the antithesis of Nel. She lives in a house whose architect is her own independent grandmother, Eva Peace. Instead of four Virgin Marys, her house has "four sickle pear trees" (30). The spectre of feminine respectability is spared Sula by her widowed mother Hannah, whose expression of sexuality is unencumbered by marital laws and expectations. However, divergent familial influences notwithstanding, Nel and Sula are both regulated by the bottom lines and patriarchal laws of acceptability drawn for women. Much of the anguish that women in Morrison's novels experience arises from a curtailment of their power. Unlike many white women, whose lives were defined by the private domain of home and family, the majority of black women had, for historical reasons, greater access to the public sphere of work. Yet this access has not necessarily brought them greater control of their lives. Like working-class women in other patriarchal societies, they have "culturally and ideologically accepted the power and control of their men, however powerless or oppressed the latter may be outside the home."[7]

---

7. Vasantha Kannabiran and K. Lalitha, "That Magic Time: Women in the Telengana People's Struggle," in *Recasting Women: Essays in Colonial History*, ed. Kumkum Sangari and Sudesh Vaid (New Delhi, 1989), 185.

This abdication of power in deference to the traditionally sanctioned power of men is more remarkable in the case of Eva, whose husband (with the telling name of Boyboy) leaves her to fend for herself and their three children. In what is a literal twist to the meaning of a self-sacrificing mother, she mutilates her own leg for an insurance legacy. And still this survivor who is the builder of her own house—and an architect of several other lives besides—is all for the obeisance of women to men. In her adherence to a norm that she herself has not lived by, Eva threatens the very being of her granddaughter Sula, who upon returning from college is interrogated by the crone:

> "When you gone to get married? You need to have some babies. It'll settle you."
> "I don't want to make somebody else. I want to make myself."
> "Selfish. Ain't no woman got no business floatin' around without no man."
> "You did."
> "Not by choice."
> "Mamma did."
> "Not by choice, I said. It ain't right for you to want to stay off by yourself. You need
> . . . I'm a tell you what you need." (92)

The critical difference between Eva and Sula is that the older woman had her power thrust on her by bitter circumstance, and she bore both a deep pride and a bitter grudge for bearing that burden. Sula, on the other hand, wants to find and exert the power of her own life, a choice the older generation of women did not have. It is also a choice the Bottom as a collective does not have. For Sula, putting her grandmother away in an old age home becomes an act of self-preservation encouraged by Eva's domineering behavior; to the community it is a scandal. Cast in the position of a heretic, cut off from the sustenance of ancestral/maternal connectedness, Sula finds herself in social limbo.

Part of the lovelessness that is Sula's lot is also history's unsentimental legacy to her, one that is passed via her mother Hannah, who inherited it from Eva. Of Hannah we know little, but beyond the gentle, earthy woman—whose funky, loose ways could be both complimentary and maddening to women who had their husbands to guard—we glimpse a shade of silence. We know that she "ended up a daylight lover," that she would not *sleep* with the men, for it "implied for her a measure of trust and a definite commitment," neither of which she felt. We know from the question she poses to Eva in 1923 that as a daughter she lacked maternal nurturing: "Mamma, did you ever love us?" Such questions are frequently posed by a younger generation removed from crisis, freed to contemplate questions other than those dictated by the exigencies of survival that occupied the previous generation. The older generation perceives such queries as foolish and self-indulgent, as an outrageous affront to their lives. The incomprehension on both sides is evident in the following confrontation between mother and daughter:

"You settin' here with your healthy-ass self and ax me did I love you? Them big old eyes in your head would a been two holes full of maggots if I hadn't."

"I didn't mean that, Mamma. I know you fed us and all. I was talkin' 'bout something else. Like. Like. Playin' with us. Did you ever, you know, play with us?"

"Play? Wasn't nobody playin' in 1895. Just 'cause you got it good now you think it was always this good? 1895 was a killer, girl. Things was bad. Niggers was dying like flies. Stepping tall, ain't you? Uncle Paul gone bring me *two* bushels. Yeh. And they's a melon downstairs, ain't they? And I bake every Saturday, and Shad brings fish on Friday, and they's a pork barrel. . . ."

"Mamma, what you talkin' 'bout?"

"I'm talkin' about 18 and 95 when I set in that house five days with you and Pearl and Plum and three beets, you snake-eyed ungrateful hussy. What would I look like leapin' 'round that little old room playin' with youngins with three beets to my name?" . . .

"But Mamma, they had to be some time when you wasn't thinkin' 'bout . . ."

"No time. They wasn't no time. Not none. Soon as I got one day done here come a night. With you all coughin' and me watchin' so TB wouldn't take you off. . . . What you talkin' 'bout did I love you girl I stayed alive for you can't you get that through your thick head or what is that between your ears, heifer?" (68–69)

Truth is harsh, and Eva, a survivor of that deadly winter of 1895, is incapable of softening it, of comprehending Hannah's plea for love. The roughness of her own hardships have made Eva insensitive and intolerant to others' vulnerabilities and needs.

To her soldier son Plum, defeated by war, Eva's reaction carries to the extreme the sort of mother's response given in Langston Hughes's poem "Mother to Son":

I'se been a climbin' on,
And reachin' landin's,
And turnin' corners,

And sometimes goin' in the dark
Where there ain't been no light,
So boy, don't you turn back.
Don't you set down on the steps
'Cause you finds it kinder hard.[8]

Plum returns home from war in a state of shock similar to Shadrack's, but unlike the latter, he is unable to pull himself together, withdrawing into the oblivion of drugs. Witnessing his defeat is more than Eva, herself a survivor, can bear. Pronouncing him unfit to live, Eva takes his life with her own hands, thereby freeing him, and herself, from misery. In a way, Eva's dousing the helpless Plum with kerosene and setting him on fire lest he climb the regressive stairs back to her womb is a measure of what she has done to herself in order to survive. Because Eva's survival has come at the price of bodily and psychic violence, because she suppresses her own great vulnerability by the sheer force of will to survive, she cannot bear to see vulnerability in her son. Her need to control the threat of chaos is evident in her adoption and naming of the three little boys she calls "Deweys." They remain infantile and at her mercy, never growing up into self-reliant adults. In sending Plum to his death, she demonstrates her own desperate mastery of defeat. But this is a brittle mastery. Having sacrificed her life for the well-being of her children, Eva is compelled to burn her son and forced to watch her daughter Hannah burn.

History and ancestry bear on the present. Sula exhibits Eva's characteristic response to life when she and Nel are threatened with the danger of molestation by some Irish boys: desperately slashing her finger with a knife before their eyes, she says, "If I can do that to myself, what you suppose I'll do to you?" The loving care denied Hannah in 1895 has its repercussions in the next generation. Sula nonchalantly watches as her mother goes up in flames. One can only guess from her bystander's reaction to Hannah's death that Sula has lacked from Hannah what Hannah lacked from Eva. Of course, the burden of history falls inevitably on the black woman as mother—as Eva protests, "Everybody all right. 'Cept Mamma. Mamma the only one ain't all right. Cause she didn't *love* us." Each generation's struggle is different and relatively incomprehensible to the next.

8. Langston Hughes, "Mother to Son," *Selected Poems of Langston Hughes* (New York, 1974), 187.

We leave Sula on her death bed, which was also Eva's bed—a "sturdy termination" of generations of struggle. Eventually both come up against a boarded-up window, a "sealed," "blind window" beyond which they cannot see or go (148). Here Sula enters "a sleep full of dreams of cobalt blue," a color signifying the open sky of possibilities, a vision yet to be. She becomes aware that she has "sung all the songs there are." The last image of Sula is a symbolic one; we see her as she does herself, as an embryonic form voyaging toward a new birth: "held by this blind window . . . [at last] she might draw her legs up to her chest, close her eyes, put her thumb in her mouth and float over and down the tunnels, just missing the dark walls, down, down until she met a rain scent and would know the water was near, and she would curl into its heavy softness and it would envelop her, carry her, and wash her tired flesh always. Always" (137). This desire to return to the matrix of the womb and the longing for maternal nurturing (in the verbs *envelop, carry, wash*) accent an important subtext in the novel.

Social drama is the term cultural anthropologist Victor Turner employs to highlight the relations of power in a given community. Social dramas consist of episodes of conflict "when the interests and attitudes of groups and individuals [stand] in obvious opposition." Not surprisingly, Turner finds that the relationships involved in social drama are "structural relationships," those "concerned mainly with relations between persons in their status-role capacity" pertaining to "servitude to structural rights and obligations, imperatives, and loyalties." Contrary to bonds of structure are those of *communitas*: these are the "undifferentiated, equalitarian, direct, nonrational (though not *ir*rational), I-Thou or Essential We relationships, in Martin Buber's sense." As Turner observes, relations of structure and communitas are two "human modes" not mutually exclusive but whose balanced coexistence has always been a "perennial human social problem."[9] Sula's life can be read as one woman's search for communitas in a community where women's lives are organized by imperatives of structure.

It is communitas that characterizes the relationship that Sula and Nel—girls relatively unconstrained by the structural roles of womanhood—experi-

9. Victor Turner, *Dramas, Fields, and Metaphors: Symbolic Action in Human Society* (Ithaca, N.Y., 1974), 33, 45–46, 266.

ence together: "In the safe harbor of each other's company they could afford to abandon the ways of other people and concentrate on their own perception of things" (55). The lives of most women in the Bottom are ridden with structural constraints of marital and maternal duties, circumscribed as their lives are by the frustrations of a racially demarcated poverty. Upon her return to the Bottom, Sula reflects on the women she knew:

> She could not say to those old acquaintances, "Hey, girl, you looking good," when she saw how the years had dusted their bronze with ash, the eyes that had once opened wide to the moon bent into grimy sickles of concern. The narrower their lives, the wider their hips. Those with husbands had folded themselves into starched coffins. . . . Those without men were like sour-tipped needles featuring one constant empty eye. Those with men had had the sweetness sucked from their breath by ovens and steam kettles. . . . They had looked at the world and back at their children, and Sula knew that one clear young eye was all that kept the knife away from the throat's curve. (121–122)

They are the kin of Jean Toomer's mournful women, of Alice Walker's bleeding, martyred women artists. In the Bottom, Sula alone refuses such a reality, which is not simply a function of poverty, but also of gender roles. Sula and Nel's estrangement highlights the process by which socially engendered constraints are personally internalized by women. Sula ruefully reflects on the achievement and loss of communitas with Nel:

> Nel was the one person who had wanted nothing from her, who had accepted all aspects of her. . . . Nel was the first person who had been real to her, whose name she knew, who had seen as she had the slant of life that made it possible to stretch it to its limits. Now Nel was one of them. One of the spiders whose only thought was the next rung of the web, who dangled in dark dry places suspended by their own spittle, more terrified of the free fall than the snake's breath below. . . . If they were touched by the snake's breath, however fatal, they were merely victims and knew how to behave in that role (just as Nel knew how to behave as the wronged wife). But the free fall, oh no, that required—demanded—invention: a thing to do with the wings, a way of holding the legs and most of all a surrender to the downward flight if they wished to taste their tongues or stay alive. But alive was what they, and now Nel, did not want to be. Too dangerous. (119–120)

The creation of communitas calls for a struggle, the invention of a new social order signaled by feminism. While both Nel and Sula are subject to the limitations of the existing social structures, Sula has the distinction of daring to risk the free fall from the social web of proscriptions.

Sula's failure to find communitas in heterosexual relationships attests to the imbalance of power that structures male and female identities. This gendered imbalance is illustrated in Sula's relationship with Ajax, which begins with the promise of comradeship but ends with the unexpected but not surprising emergence of structural differences. Turner suggests that "we regard sexuality . . . as the expression, in its various modalities, either of communitas or of structure": "Sexuality, as a biological drive, is culturally and hence symbolically manipulated to express one or the other of these major dimensions of sociality. It thus becomes a means to social ends, quite as much as an end to which social means are contrived. Whereas structure emphasizes, and even exaggerates, the biological differences between the sexes, in matters of dress, decoration, and behavior, communitas tends to diminish these diferences."[10] Until she meets Ajax, Sula has subjected herself to a host of male lovers in a vain search for reciprocity. Instead she encounters "a stinging awareness of the endings of things" and "an eye of sorrow" (123). Ajax is a welcome exception. There is the potential of a profound comradeship; unlike Jude, who absorbs Nel into himself, Ajax is not interested in he and Sula making one Ajax. Yet the asymmetries of power disrupt their brief association, rendering them incomprehensible to each other.

If communitas "is a relationship between concrete, historical, idiosyncratic individuals," "a direct, immediate and total confrontation of human identities," then structure "is all that holds people apart, defines their differences, and constrains their actions."[11] A disfranchised black man outside the white man's economy and the law, Ajax cannot fulfill his desire to fly airplanes, yet he is at home in the community of the Bottom, which nurses his wounds. Women fight each other for him, his mother nurtures him without demands, he does not have to answer to anything but his own whims, and certainly nobody castigates him for the relationships he does or does not have. This, however, is not the case with Sula. Though she has ventured outside her community and become worldly wise, inside the community she steps into the sheltered space of her

10. *Ibid.*, 247.
11. *Ibid.*, 47.

mother's house; outside it, there is no place for her. Because of the sexual liberties she takes, her status in the community is liminal. From his makeshift, male-centered world, Ajax cannot relate to her lonesome predicament. Sula's invitation to him to lean on her signals to him her need to claim him. Sensing in her a proclivity for "the nest," Ajax leaves Sula. While his rejection of Sula signifies his rejection of the structural imperatives of being a man (which he recognizes as an impossibility), his departure also signifies his inability to iden-tify with Sula's own rejection of the structural imperatives of gender roles in her life. He is not a comrade. So, on her deathbed, it is not Ajax that she recalls. Instead, she thinks of a kindred pariah, Shadrack. And she dies thinking of Nel, whom she regards as her comrade despite their rift. For her part, Nel discovers that her years of loyalty and sacrifice to her marriage to Jude have not amounted to anything apart from begetting children, the responsibility for whom rests squarely with her.

The private griefs of Sula and Nel exemplify the feminist dictum that the personal is the political. Shadrack, the shell-shocked World War I veteran, is Sula's comrade-in-arms who resists the privatization of madness by ritualizing a national suicide day. The power of Morrison's writing stems from her ability to fill the insidious gap that Fredric Jameson labels in *The Political Unconscious* as "that structural, experiential, and conceptual gap between the public and the private, between history or society and the 'individual,' which—the ten-dential law of social life under capitalism—maims our existence as individual subjects and paralyzes our thinking about time and change just as surely as it alienates us from our speech itself."[12] Returned from the war in France, Shadrack experiences this conceptual paralysis, the hiatus between the public and pri-vate, when he is coming to consciousness after lying comatose for months in the hospital. The social order contains those it violates with a straitjacket labeled "private." More difficult than the physical coordinating of his hands and body is the making sense of his reality: "Laced and silent in his small bed, he tried to tie the loose cords in his mind. He wanted desperately to see his own face and connect it with the word 'private'—the word the nurse (and the others who helped bind him) had called him. 'Private' he thought was some-thing secret, and he wondered why they looked at him and called him a se-

---

12. Fredric Jameson, *The Political Unconscious: Narrative as a Socially Symbolic Act* (Ithaca, N.Y., 1981), 20.

cret" (10). To call him Private is to hail the traumatic condition of Shadrack, the public insanity of war, as one of his own making.

From their reading of Kafka, Deleuze and Guattari made certain extrapolations about minor literature, "that which a minority constructs within a major language." According to them, one of the main characteristics of minor literatures is that "everything in them is political. In major literatures, in contrast, the individual concern (familial, marital, and so on) joins with other no less individual concerns, the social milieu serving as a mere environment or a background. . . . Minor literature is completely different; its cramped space forces each individual intrigue to connect immediately to politics. The individual concern thus becomes all the more necessary, indispensable, because a whole other story is vibrating within it."[13] In *Sula* the familial and marital concern does not remain simply individual, because indeed "a whole other story is vibrating within it." There is nothing mysterious about this. If the individual is affiliated with a group whose location in the social structure is marginal (Jews for Kafka, black people for Morrison), and if the individual's (black woman's) location both within and outside the group is historically unsatisfactory, the individual concerns must be articulated in a manner that puts into crisis the *entire* social structure. Minor literature is compelled to make the politically unconscious conscious.

Addressing intertextuality, Monique Wittig remarks: "In history, in politics, one is dependent on social history, while in one's work a writer is dependent on literary history, that is, on the history of forms. What is at the center of history and politics is the social body, constituted by the people. What is at the center of literature is forms, constituted by works."[14] *Sula* can be situated intertextually among two modernist literary works whose themes the novel evokes and revises. It invites a comparison with Virginia Woolf's *Mrs. Dalloway* and T. S. Eliot's *The Waste Land*, both of which address time, death, memory, and madness, the great themes of the modernist sublime, themes that are given a singularly African American expression in *Sula*.

Shadrack has a brother and forerunner-in-arms, Septimus Warren Smith, in *Mrs. Dalloway*, a novel that addresses the period in British life directly after

13. Deleuze and Guattari, *Toward a Minor Literature*, 17. See my elaboration upon minor literature in the Introduction.

14. Monique Wittig, "The Trojan Horse," *Feminist Issues* (Fall, 1984), 46.

World War I. These disturbed prophets of peace hold our gaze on the deranged center of war. While the social worlds of the two novels are diametrically opposed (Woolf's Mrs. Dalloway hobnobs with aristocrats and colonial bureaucrats in Westminster, London), both novels delineate a woman's consciousness in an alienating patriarchal world using vivid, sensuous, and lyrical prose. *Mrs. Dalloway*, following James Joyce's *Ulysses*, covers one day in June in the life of Clarissa Dalloway. The stately, loud Big Ben, heard throughout the novel, governs a masculine public sphere of administration and commerce; the clocks of Harley street "counselled submission, upheld authority."[15] In marked contrast, women's time seems private, filled with small odds and ends. In *Sula*, too, a heightened sense of time prevails. While *Mrs. Dalloway* covers the lived experience of one day, *Sula* covers four decades. Yet with all its delicate ironies and sad nuances, Woolf's novel is a celebration of life in all its aching flux: Mrs. Dalloway is, after all, throwing a party, and her elite world of Westminster—in which she is critical—is in no danger of being erased. Morrison's reproachful claim to a bleaker history renders *Sula*'s difference.

Representing female friendship, heterosexual love, and marriage, both novels raise the issue of women's alienation. In *Mrs. Dalloway*, the early relationship between Clarissa and her girlhood friend Sally Seton is comparable to the friendship of Sula and Nel. Here is Clarissa reminiscing about Sally:

The strange thing, on looking back, was the purity, the integrity, of her feeling for Sally. It was not like one's feeling for a man. It was completely disinterested, and besides, it had a quality which could only exist between women, between women just grown up. It was protective, on her side; sprang from a sense of being in league together, a presentiment of something that was bound to part them (they spoke of marriage always as a catastrophe), which led to this chivalry, this protective feeling which was more on her side than Sally's. For in those days she was completely reckless; did the most idiotic things out of bravado. . . . But the charm was overpowering. . . . she could remember going cold with excitement, and doing her hair in a kind of ecstacy . . . all because she was coming down to dinner in a white frock to meet Sally Seton![16]

These reflections may well serve as a description of the friendship between Sula and Nel "whose friendship was as intense as it was sudden." We are told "they found relief in each other's personality" and "found in each other's eyes the

15. Virginia Woolf, *Mrs. Dalloway* (London, 1925), 154.
16. *Ibid.*, 50–51.

intimacy they were looking for," each having "discovered years before that they were neither white nor male, and that all freedom and triumph was forbidden to them" (52–53). *Sula*, as if drawing out the subtext of Woolf's novel, is an interrogation of all that makes women's friendships with other women secondary to their relationships with men. Unlike Clarissa's early awareness of Sally, Nel does not know how much she values Sula until much after Sula's death. However, her belated cry of recognition at the end of the novel serves to highlight the significance of their relationship. In *Sula*, the pain of a love (Nel's) directed toward an absence (Sula's) is both visceral and stunning. It seems fair to say that the composite limitations of being black and female and relegated to the bottom of the social hierarchy make *Sula* a more anguished novel than *Mrs. Dalloway*, whose central character, married to a colonial bureaucrat, moves in the upper echelons of society. Further, if after Deleuze and Guattari we may see Virginia Woolf's writing as a kind of minor literature operating within the major language of English men, Toni Morrison signifies on her literary foremother in another minor practice.

The somber mood of *Sula* has some affinity with T. S. Eliot's *The Waste Land*, whose title descriptor applies well to the Bottom. The novel resurrects certain phrases, motifs, and images from the master poem for its own intense signifying practice. Mixing memory and desire, it echoes the poem's multiple deaths: the poem's "burial of the dead," "death by water," and "burning" find their correspondences in *Sula*. It is tempting to see Shadrack as the wounded Fisher King, the ritual healer associated with the river and fish as a symbol of regeneration, just as his name associates him with the fiery furnace from which the "Lord pluckest [him] burning."[17] If *The Waste Land* is a personalized expression of the all-pervasive angst attending the destruction of World War I, *Sula* expresses the long and slow death of hope in a black community, the trials of black women and black men who fought the war and suffered its disorder ever after. The images of communal life in the Bottom are the fragments Morrison shores against its ruins.

In *Sula*, the metaphor of the waste land is given a final cutting social commentary. At the end of the novel, the reader is shown to "the colored part of the cemetery" in Beechnut Park, to the carved slabs beneath which Sula and her family lie: "Together they read like a chant: PEACE 1895–1921, PEACE 1890–1923, PEACE 1910–1940, PEACE 1892–1959. They were not dead people. They

17. T. S. Eliot, "The Waste Land," *Selected Poems* (London, 1976), 49–74.

were words. Not even words. Wishes, longings" (171). Readers of *The Waste Land* know that the poem ends with the Sanskrit chant for peace, "Shantih, Shantih, Shantih." Morrison's "chant" of Peace vis-à-vis Eliot's has the function of "competing metaphors," metaphors competing with one another to "demonstrate what their own and the other's boundaries are, what insights they offer, and what blindnesses they suffer."[18] For Morrison, peace is what the black folk of the Bottom have lacked and longed for from 1895 to 1959; peace is not something that existed and was then disrupted by World War I. It has been absent from the beginning.

18. Paul B. Armstrong, *Conflicting Readings: Variety and Validity in Interpretation* (Chapel Hill, N.C., 1990), 82.

3

REDEEMING THE LEGACY OF THE PAST:
Song of Solomon

The past carries with it a temporal index by which it is referred
to redemption. There is a secret agreement between past
generations and the present one. . . . Like every generation
that preceded us, we have been endowed with a *weak*
Messianic power, a power to which the past has a claim.
—Walter Benjamin, "Theses on the
Philosophy of History"

Historical responsibility has, after all, to do with action—
where we place the weight of our existences on the line, cast
our lot with others, move from an individual consciousness to
a collective one.
—Adrienne Rich, "Resisting Amnesia:
History and Personal Life"

Reading *Song of Solomon*, W. Lawrence Hogue charges Morrison with
"rendering middle-class life as perverted, grotesque, atomizing, emotionally,
spiritually, and sexually dead," and with withholding "attractive or positive
images of this class"—a strategic rendering that serves "to deny [middle-class
life] as a possible alternative for Milkman and the reader."[1] Let us note, however,
that Milkman is (and remains) middle class. What he does not remain by the
end of the novel is a complacent and preoccupied male member of that class.
The historic role of the middle class is accomodating; the role of the upper-

. W. Lawrence Hogue, *Race, Modernity, Postmodernity: A Look at the History and the Literatures
of People of Color Since the 1960s* (New York, 1996), 37.

middle-class—where Hogue places Milkman—is conservative, having to do with the consolidation of its material gains. In the novel, ownership of things, the creed and credo of Milkman's father, Macon Dead, is juxtaposed with his aunt's lack of ownership of anything or anyone other than her own name. Morrison is mediating a split identity, a family quarrel not just between brother Macon and sister Pilate but between northern urban black mobility and the jettisoned southern past. The title of the novel hearkens back to the blues tradition that Macon has left behind and Pilate has kept. A song is what Pilate offers her nephew, a song that is a register of historic and cultural memory, which revises for Milkman the very field of his middle-class identifications.

Milkman's tutelage under Aunt Pilate, her turning him toward the past, becomes a question of reconstituting his values. Michael Lambek posits memory as more than just the remembering of "the temporal dimension of experience"; memory is also "a culturally mediated expression . . . of social commitments and identifications." Memory constructs identity; following Charles Taylor, Lambek notes that "the chronotrope of memory" is also "a moral space." According to Charles Taylor, a moral orientation is linked to identity: "To know who you are is to be oriented in moral space, a space in which questions arise about what is good or bad, what is worth doing and what not, what has meaning and importance for you and what is trivial and secondary."[2]

Central to Morrison's reclamatory project of storytelling is the forging of Milkman Dead's identification with the historically shaped meaning of blackness. Milkman's is the eventual attainment of what W. E. B. Du Bois calls "self-conscious manhood," the "[merging of] his double self into a better and truer self." This double self or "twoness" that Du Bois alludes to is the presence of "two warring ideals in one dark body": "an American, a Negro." Morrison addresses these "unreconciled strivings" by resolutely teaching her middle-class protagonist not to "bleach his Negro soul in a flood of white Americanism". Commenting on Du Bois's statement of double consciousness, Arnold Rampersad provides this insight: "Another way of seeing these two souls surely is as a contest between memory and its opposite, amnesia. American culture demands of its blacks amnesia concerning slavery and Africa, just as it encourages amnesia of a different kind in whites."[3] The implications of remembering are

2. Michael Lambek, "The Past Imperfect: Remembering as Moral Practice," in *Tense Past*, ed. Antze and Lambek 248–49; Charles Taylor, qtd. in Lambek, 249.

3. Du Bois, *The Souls of Black Folk*, 45; Arnold Rampersad, "Du Bois's *The Souls of Black Folk*,"

well clarified by Jewish American feminist poet Adrienne Rich in the epigraph above. *Song of Solomon* may be read as a counter-*Bildungsroman* whose mission is the development of a historical and ethical consciousness in the bourgeois character of Milkman Dead.

Although the protagonist is male, the novel reassesses the legacy of the forefathers from Pilate's—a daughter's—perspective. This perspective enables the novel to offer a critique of the repressive law of the father. Morrison describes *Song of Solomon* as "a journey from stupidity to epiphany, of a man, a complete man." Crucial to this development is Milkman's learning to respect black women and to establish a relationship of reciprocity with them. He is spurred on to his journey toward maturity by his sister Lena's furious ultimatum: "You are a sad, pitiful, stupid, selfish, hateful man. I hope your little hog's gut stands you in good stead, and that you take good care of it, because you don't have anything else. But I want to give you notice."[4]

The first part of the novel, set in the North, makes us experience Milkman's life of partial narratives; the second half takes us back to the South, where the present can be related to the past and where Milkman can piece together all his stories to make a single, meaningful narrative. Adrienne Rich has warned against "the trope of linearity," which construes progress as forward movement in terms of the distance achieved from the past: "We become less dimensional than we really are. The dialectic between change and continuity is a painful but deeply instructive one, in personal life as in the life of a people. To 'see the light' too often has meant rejecting the treasures found in darkness."[5] Informed by a similar critique, Morrison chose a narrative structure that is cyclical. *Song* develops its meaning through the trope of a progressive return to the past. Linearity ends in Part I not in progress but in stasis, with thirty-one-year-old Milkman at the end of his spiritual tether.

Song of Solomon revolts against its own "birthplace" as characterized by Walter Benjamin: "The art of storytelling is reaching its end because the epic side of

---

in *Slavery and the Literary Imagination*, ed. Arnold Rampersad and Deborah E. McDowell (Baltimore, 1989), 118.

4. Toni Morrison, "The Site of Memory," *Inventing the Truth: The Art and Craft of Memoir*, ed. William Zinsser (Boston, 1987), 124; Morrison, *Song of Solomon*, (New York, 1977), 218. Subsequent page references will be cited within parentheses in the text.

5. Adrienne Rich, "Resisting Amnesia: History and Personal Life," *Blood, Bread, and Poetry* (New York, 1986), 143–44.

truth, wisdom, is dying out. . . . The birthplace of the novel is the solitary individual, who is no longer able to express himself by giving examples of his most important concerns, is himself uncounseled, and cannot counsel others." While *Song of Solomon* is no doubt germinated by the isolation Benjamin identifies as being the novelist's, it is also a response to "the secular productive forces of history" that "removed narrative from the realm of living speech." Morrison takes the bourgeois art form read in isolation and transforms it so that it *does* become a performance containing counsel and wisdom. "Memory is the epic faculty *par excellence*," observes Benjamin in "The Storyteller." "Memory creates the chain of tradition which passes a happening on from generation to generation." Morrison's novel performs this linkage between generations even as it registers the griot/storyteller's demise in modernity. Milkman's aunt Pilate, a keeper of the oral tradition, dies at the end. "There's got to be at least one more woman like you," mourns Milkman at her grave (340). The novel takes the place of her absence, commemorating in print what she embodied, encoding, in Benjamin's words, "the perpetuating remembrance of the novelist" who survives the demise of the storyteller.[6]

Song of Solomon is a novel that actively reconstructs the meaning of black-ness, and as such it belongs among the group of novels that have documented and refashioned ethnic identities in the United States since the 1970s. Novels that resonate alongside Morrison's are Louise Erdrich's *Love Medicine*, in which the protagonist's reentry into the Chippewa culture parallels Milkman's claim-ing of his heritage, and Maxine Hong Kingston's *China Men*, a novel about forefathers and their forgotten legacies. Other such works include Native Amer-ican writer Leslie Marmon Silko's *Ceremony*, and *Voyages* by Armenian Amer-ican writer Peter Najerian. In these works, characters' self-hatred and angry confusion are related to a historic dispossession and to a psyche cut off from ancestral or communal wellsprings; their narratives chart a moving and pow-erful repossession of selfhood, articulating personal well-being in terms of the collective. In the context of a dominant hegemonic discourse, each of these writers is keenly aware of the political, cultural, and therapeutic function of narrative.

For them, the novel becomes a mode of retrieving a usable past as well as of documenting a history excised from dominant historiography. A heightened sense of the buried life informs *Song of Solomon*. In the following passage,

6. Benjamin, *Illuminations*, 87, 97–98.

Milkman, returning home from the South, "looked out the [bus] window" and "read the road signs with interest now, wondering what lay beneath the names":

How many dead lives and fading memories were buried in and beneath the names of the places in this country. Under the recorded names were other names, just as "Macon Dead," recorded for all time in some dusty file, hid from view the real names of people, places, and things. Names that had meaning. No wonder Pilate put hers in her ear. . . . He closed his eyes and thought of the black men in Shalimar, Roanoke, Petersburg . . . on Darling Street, in the pool halls, the barbershops. Their names. Names they got from yearnings, gestures, flaws, events, mistakes, weaknesses. Names that bore witness. (333)

Buried beneath the "Dead" name is a wealth of knowledge that could free the Dead to live, but Macon Dead is obsessed only with the gold buried beneath a dead man in a cave on his father's lost property. Macon's sister Pilate's sack of bones links gold to the metaphoric wealth—the spiritual, cultural, ancestral lore—of the past. Buried beneath his own name is a usable past that propels Milkman to a visionary flight instead of a blind one. In the old-fashioned words of Carl Jung, we need to "connect the life of the past that still exists in us with the life of the present, which threatens to slip away from it. If this link-up does not take place, a kind of rootless consciousness comes into being no longer oriented to the past, a consciousness which succumbs helplessly to all manner of suggestions and, in practice, is susceptible to psychic epidemics. With the loss of the past, now become 'insignificant,' devalued, and incapable of revaluation, the saviour is lost too, for the saviour is either the insignificant thing itself or else arises out of it."[7] This is also the redemptive pact between generations that Benjamin alludes to in the epigraph to this chapter.

Native American writer Leslie Silko begins her novel *Ceremony*, published in 1977, the same year as *Song of Solomon*, with an old man's revelation:

I will tell you something about stories,
[he said]
They aren't just entertainment.
Don't be fooled.
They are all we have, you see,

7. Carl Gustav Jung, *The Archetypes and the Collective Unconscious* (Princeton, N.J., 1969), 157.

all we have to fight off
illness and death
You don't have anything
if you don't have the stories.

Novels like *Song of Solomon* and *Ceremony* attempt to close the gap between the disparate worlds of print literature and oral traditions. Walter Benjamin comments on the distinction between literate and oral forms of storytelling: "What differentiates the novel from all other forms of prose literature—the fairy tale, the legend, even the novella—is that it neither comes from oral tradition nor goes into it. This distinguishes it from storytelling in particular. The storyteller takes what he tells from experience—his own or that reported by others. And he in turn makes it the experience of those who are listening to his tale." *Song of Solomon*, however, is both informed by an oral tradition and "goes into it." The story of ancestral flight that structures the novel belongs to the oral tradition, one specific to Gullah slaves of coastal Georgia and South Carolina. The following story, contained in the Georgia Writers' collection of folklore, is well-known: some African slaves, who were not broken into slavery, refused to labor, choosing to sit under a tree rather than hoe. Then came along the slave driver: "The dribuh say 'Wut dis? and dey say, Kum buba yali kum buba tambe, Kum kunka yali kum kunka tambe,' quickly like. Den dey rise off duh groun an fly away. Nobody ebuh see um no mo. Some say dey fly back tuh Africa. Muh gran see dat wid he own eye." Robert Hayden's poem "O Daedalus, Fly Away Home," is based on this story: "My gran, he flew back to Africa, / just spread his arms and / flew away home." Morrison appropriates folk tales and myths of several origins, drawing on Anglo-Saxon fairy tales, biblical stories, and Greek epics in order to engage and instruct the reader's imagination. Operating on several registers, *Song of Solomon* demonstrates, in Trinh Minh-ha's words, that "the story as a cure and a protection is at once musical, historical, poetical, ethical, educational, magical, and religious."[8]

The figure of the mother is secondary in this novel about daughters and sons relating to fathers, patronyms, and paternal legacies. (Pilate is born without a

8. Leslie Marmon Silko, *Ceremony* (New York, 1977), 2; Benjamin, *Illuminations*, 87; Georgia Writers' Project, *Drums and Shadows* (Westport, Conn., 1976), 79; Robert Hayden, *Angle of Ascent: New and Selected Poems* (New York, 1975), 124; Trinh T. Minh-ha, *Woman, Native, Other: Writing Postcoloniality and Literature* (Bloomington, Ind., 1989), 140.

navel, without a living mother; Milkman's maternal grandmother is not spoken of.) Milkman's mother, Ruth, and aunt Pilate offer two versions of the daughter's veneration for the dead father, while Macon Dead and his sister Pilate offer competing versions of paternal legacy and radically different ways of being responsible to the past. Both Macon and Ruth remember their fathers neurotically. Ruth's relation to her own father, the light-skinned Dr. Foster, has the suggestion of being incestuous and, after his death, necrophilic. Macon's memory of his murdered father drives both his need to possess property and his punishing behavior toward others. Milkman's friend Guitar, whose father "got sliced up in a sawmill" and for whose death the boss compensated by giving the children "some candy" (61), also remembers his father in pathological ways. He vents his early hatred of white people by becoming a member of a death squad meant to avenge the racist killings of black children.

Without historical perspective, Milkman is brought up short by the atmosphere of hostility and futility that surrounds him. As such he is representative of every person's existential predicament: that of being born to a time and place in medias res. With only a partial understanding of the ongoing saga preceding one, one continues to add to it, unaware of the full import of this addition. Milkman has grown up within the specific cultural discontinuity created by migration from the South to the urban North and by the black middle-class's repudiation of a stigmatized past. Macon Dead, following the theft of his father's land by white men during the violent post-Reconstruction era, has moved north to Michigan where he becomes a rich slum lord extorting rent from black people and evicting into the streets the poor (such as Mrs. Bains and her grandson Guitar) when they cannot pay. Clutching the keys to his property, he has lost the keys to well-being—his own, his family's, and his community's.

In developing the narrative of Milkman's paternal grandfather, Morrison returns to the story of Solomon Willis, her own maternal grandfather who lost his land to white intimidation and takeover. Morrison, like Pilate, also mourns the loss of her father, whose death serves as the emotional pretext of this novel concerned with fathers and their legacies. Interestingly, Morrison begins the novel at the time of her own birth, February 18, 1931. The novel's first scene opens with the suicide note of North Carolina Mutual Life Insurance agent Robert Smith: "At 3:00 P.M. on Wednesday the 18th of February, 1931, I will take off from Mercy and fly away on my own wings" (3). The next day Milkman Dead is born, and the challenge of his life is augured by this suicide: his task will be to grasp the meaning of the sociohistoric context of his birth and, because the "gift of continuity carries its own burdens with it," to transcend the fatality of despair and hatred by becoming an agent who insures mutual life.[9]

Milkman's life is surrounded by death wishes: Milkman's unloved mother, Ruth, tried unsuccessfully to abort him, his lover Hagar goes after him with a knife, and his friend Guitar is out to kill him. In short, his very life is imperiled, and he himself submits to the death wish: "Milkman lay quietly in the sunlight, his mind a blank, his lungs craving smoke. Gradually his fear of and eagerness for death returned. Above all he wanted to escape what he knew, escape the implications of what he had been told. . . . He felt like a garbage pail for the actions and hatreds of other people. He himself did nothing . . . he felt put upon; felt as though some burden had been given to him and that he didn't deserve it. None of that was his fault" (120). He is rescued by his outlawed aunt Pilate Dead whose name, though doubly associated with death (the Roman Pontius Pilate presided over the trial of Jesus before the Crucifixion), is allied with the principle of redemption, here defined as the life-sustaining connection with the past. Through Milkman the novel shows, in Adrienne Rich's words, that we are "born both innocent and accountable" and "cannot help making history because we are made of it"; what we can do is choose whether or not to "become *consciously* historical."[10] If the living present in the novel is full of dead ends, the dead past is still living in names, in places, in fragments of folklore, in characters' unconscious motives. The question becomes how to lift the repressions of the present, how to honor the dead in conscious rituals of burial and remembrance that vouchsafe the proper communion between the living and the dead.

The novel's epigraph contains the line, "And the children may know their names." Milkman's family name is significant in more ways than one: first, because it falsifies their origins as well as the identities thrust upon them by a federal agent, the name is a living testimony to the dominant culture's disregard of any history or identity other than its own; second, it signifies the attitude of the black middle class toward the slave past: they would rather consign it to oblivion than let it persist as a humiliating reminder. Milkman's grandfather accepts a name that would "wipe out the past" (54) and give him a clean start;

9. Joan Nestle, qtd. in Rich, *Blood, Bread, and Poetry,* 142.
10. Rich, *Blood, Bread, and Poetry,* 144–45.

in doing so Milkman becomes heir to a historical amnesia that is culturally and pyschically debilitating—if not lethal.

Milkman Dead's first name connects him to his mother's repressed sexual life and loveless marriage; spurned by her husband Macon, Ruth nurses her son long after it is necessary to do so. Morrison implicates Ruth's sexual repression in her genteel class and color affiliations, which her light-skinned black father, the Doctor, was anxious to maintain. Milkman is caught in the power struggle between Macon and the privileged Doctor's daughter. If Macon is the castrated/castrating father who commands his son to align with him, Milkman is the oedipal son compelled to obey the law of the father in the neurotic search for gold. Under Pilate's influence, Milkman's first name signifies the maternal capacity to nurture, and the gold becomes the buried wealth of patronymic lore. Drawing him into the matrix of African American culture, Pilate functions as the life-ensuring mother figure for Milkman.

In the process of inscribing the past and in making it connect with the present, Morrison is also revising certain aspects of past and contemporary culture. As Renato Constantino observes, "A people's history . . . must deal with the past with a view to explaining the present. . . . It must deal not only with objective developments but also bring the discussion to the realm of value judgements."[11] Thus, this novel about a young man's growth and recovery of his patrimony also critiques the male paradigm of heroism. The power and wonder in the story of the flying African is undercut by the question "Who'd he leave behind?" (332)—a reminder of the burdens black women had to endure alone because men, preoccupied with their own escape, could not or would not shoulder them.

If the flying African ancestors' flight from slavery is an escape from responsibilities to the women and children left behind, the subsequent flight of the African American middle class is represented as another form of escape. Referring to the attitude of blacks in the late 1950s and early 1960s, Morrison notes: "In the legitimate and necessary drive for better jobs and housing, we abandoned the past and a lot of the truth and sustenance that went with it. . . . In trying to cure the cancer of slavery and its consequences, some healthy as well as malignant cells were destroyed. . . . The point is not to soak in some

---

11. Renato Constantino, qtd. in Roy Armes's *Third World Film Making and the West* (Berkeley, 1987), vii.

warm bath of nostalgia about the good old days—*there were none!*—but to recognize and rescue those qualities of resistance, excellence and integrity that were so much a part of our past and so useful to us."[12] In the novel, class mobility is described as a blind flight from history. Macon Dead's big Packard, a status symbol in which the family takes rides into the country, is fittingly called a "hearse" by black folk in the neighborhood. Milkman, seated facing the back of the car, was truly "riding backward," not forward: "It was like flying blind, and not knowing where he was going—just where he had been—troubled him" (31–32).

As Dan McAdams notes, "The problem of identity is the problem of arriving at a life story that makes sense—provides unity and purpose—within a socio-historical matrix that embodies a much larger story." The blues constitute the black sociohistorical matrix in *Song of Solomon*. But as LeRoi Jones wryly documents in his history of black music, "the middle-class Negroes had gotten 'free' of all the blues tradition."[13] Morrison interprets this "freedom" as cultural deprivation, vividly pictured in the scene where Macon Dead stands in the shadows outside his sister Pilate's window, listening to her sing with her daughter and granddaughter while brewing the wine they bootlegged. Macon "knew it was not food she was stirring. . . . They ate what they had or came across or had a craving for." Her singing, however, is soul food: Macon "felt the irritability of the day drain from him and relished the effortless beauty of the women singing in the candlelight" (29–30). His position as an outsider to this spiritually sustaining world is a reminder of the price of middle-class respectability.

Against "the persistent calls to oblivion made by the mainstream of the society," the blues constitute, according to LeRoi Jones, "the peculiar social, cultural, economic, and emotional experience of a black man in America." For Milkman, then, initiation into blues is "a kind of ethno-historic rite as basic as blood." Angela Davis points out that in the postslavery years African American women musicians would impart through music "a collective consciousness and a very specific communal yearning for freedom."[14]

12. Morrison, "Rediscovering Black History," 14.

13. Dan P. McAdams, *Power, Intimacy, and the Life Story: Personological Inquiries into Identity* (New York, 1988), 18; Jones, *Blues People*, 176.

14. Jones, *Blues People*, 131, 147; Angela Davis, "Black Women and Music: A Historical Legacy of Struggle," in *Wild Women in the Whirlwind: Afra-American Literature and the Contemporary Literary Renaissance*, ed. Joanne M. Braxton and Andrée Nicola McLaughlin (New Brunswick, N.J., 1990), 6, 10.

Morrison admits that she hopes to have her fiction do "what the music did for blacks." *Song of Solomon* intends to save or keep alive by inscribing in print the unifying force of aural/oral forms such as music and storytelling. The novel's opening scene is a strategic one in this respect. Accompanying the highly visual and dramatic description of the black insurance agent's suicide is the "powerful contralto" of Pilate's blues song:

O Sugarman done fly away
Sugarman done gone
Sugarman cut across the sky
Sugarman gone home. . . . (5)

Pilate's blues song and its referent, the historic/mythic flying African, depicts the despairing Robert Smith with blue silk wings; it succeeds in unifying, in "an Afro-American expressive field" (Houston Baker's phrase), people as far removed from each other as the genteel Ruth Foster Dead and the poor Mrs. Bains, Guitar's mother. Divided by class and color lines, the fellow citizens of Afro-America come together in a nationalist composition of red (velvet rose petals), white (the snow she spills them on), and blue (silk wings).

Yet, as Morrison notes, "The music kept us alive, but it's not enough anymore."[15] The implication is that the younger generation growing up in the urban industrial cities of the North, in a culture of mass commodification, are not able to withstand alienation. Pilate loses her granddaughter, Hagar, to the materialism and cultural displacement in the North. Hagar lacks a communal support system just as Pauline Breedlove, displaced from Alabama, lacks one in Lorain, Ohio, in *The Bluest Eye*. Even Pilate's rootedness and love are unable to shield Hagar from the devaluation of black identity. But despite these somber elements, the novel is buoyed by its mission of retrieving the knowledge of the past. Pilate's death underscores the necessity of the recuperation of the dying heritage.

The family quarrel between Macon and Pilate Dead, symbolic of the rifts in black identities and allegiances, have repercussions in the next generation. The deadly tension between Milkman and Guitar, the alienated relationship between the middle class and the working class, is presided over by Pilate, the very matrix of black culture—one that is dying. The novel closes with an

15. Morrison, "The Language Must Not Sweat," 121.

allegorical tableau: as Pilate is dying from the wound inflicted by Guitar, Milkman inherits her song and turns to the blues matrix from which he was disconnected. We witness in the "blood oozing from [Pilate's] neck into his cupped hand," in the "darkness staining his hand," a cultural transfusion and transference, a culture's insurance against death (340).

The central challenge and dilemma concerning the issue of ethnicity in America is, as Werner Sollors puts it, how to avoid "the Scylla of (self-hating) assimilationism and the Charybdis of (aggressively antiwhite) nationalism." Through Milkman Dead and Guitar Bains the novel represents these national dilemmas of identity. If Milkman's problem is suggested by his name, a black identity whitened, Guitar's problem is a baneful race politics sowing discord with hate. *Song of Solomon* is a novel that strives to "avoid ethnic chauvinism and faceless universalism" while claiming what Cornel West calls the "partisan passion" for ethnic identity.[16] The polarities of black aggression and white assimilation, of discordant *tar* and faceless *milk*, had been mediated by Pilate, the custodian of black culture. Members of the urban working class and middle class, respectively, Guitar and Milkman are raised without the knowledge imparted through expressive cultural forms. Although Guitar does not play the quintessential blues instrument he is named for, he yearns for it as a child. He has been expressing his name, his potential, in truncated form: tar, blackness without the harmony. Milkman is drawn toward Pilate's house but is forbidden to interact with her by Macon Dead's middle-class scruples of propriety. Guitar, a militant black youth, is alienated from the black traditions of song, while Milkman, as his name suggests, is alienated from the story or historicity of blackness.

Guitar attempts to bridge the alienation he feels by using his restless energy for a purpose. The militant race redressing group he joins is ironically called the Seven Days—instead of creating, they destroy. By taking the lives of innocent white people each time black lives fall victim to racial prejudice, the group thinks it is doing the race a service. But Guitar, as he himself declares to Milkman, is not crazy but angry. Through him Morrison broaches the subject of black dispossession and cyclical violence more fully explored in *Jazz*. Even-

16. Werner Sollors, *Beyond Ethnicity: Consent and Descent in American Culture* (New York, 1986), 192; Cornel West, "The New Cultural Politics of Difference," *October* LIII (Summer, 1990), 108.

tually, Guitar, suspecting Milkman of hiding gold from him, turns his cold rage upon his friend. The novel places the onus of a solution on the middle-class Milkman, on the radical transformation of Milkman's heart and vision, a change brought by an understanding of his pact with the past.

In the South, Milkman undergoes a rapid series of epiphanies by which he acquires a depth of understanding and insight into his relation with others. In "the backwoods of Virginia," in a general store in Shalimar, the home town of his grandfather and grandmother, Milkman gets into a fight with a local black man, Saul. Angered by Milkman's nonchalant admission about buying a new car because the car he came in broke down, Saul forcefully impresses upon Milkman the chasm of class that separates him from his brothers in the South. Later, sitting beneath a tree in the deep night of the Virginia wilderness, Milkman returns to a deeper stratum of memory. Hearing the dialog between the local black hunters and their dogs in the still of the Blue Ridge Mountains, Milkman listens to what existed "before things were written down." He hears their communication in terms of black music: "All those shrieks, those rapid tumbling barks, the long sustained yells, the tuba sounds, the drumbeat sounds, the low liquid *howm howm*, the reedy whistles, the thin *eeeee*'s of a cornet, the *unh unh unh* bass chords. It was all language" (281). With sharpened intuition, Milkman begins to awaken to the buried lives of others: "This was what Guitar had missed about the South—the woods, hunters, killing. But something had maimed him, scarred him like Reverend Cooper's knot, like Saul's missing teeth, and like his own father. He felt a sudden rush of affection for them all, and out there under the sweet gum tree, within the sound of men tracking a bobcat, he thought he understood Guitar now. Really understood him" (282).

Milkman is finally coming home: "Down either side of his thighs he felt the sweet gum's surface roots cradling him like the rough but maternal hands of a grandfather" (281). On returning to the general store to fix his car, Milkman watches a group of black children playing and singing the blues song Pilate often sang, except instead of "Sugarman," they substitute "Solomon" and sing additional verses:

Jake the only son of Solomon
Come booba yalle, come booba tambee
Whirled about and touched the sun
Come konka yalle, come konka tambee . . . (306)

After listening attentively, Milkman realizes they are singing about his grand-father Jake, who is the son of the flying African Solomon who left behind twenty-one children and his wife, Ryna. In recovering his genealogy, he also discovers his Native American heritage. The legacy of the Native American grandmother Sing Byrd blends with the African American one of song and flight, consolidating Milkman's various identities. The novel brackets the Native American story; we are merely told that the living descendants of Heddy, Sing's mother, have all "passed" their way into white American culture.

What emerges in this novel reconstructing historical consciousness is the stultifying reality of black women's truncated lives. Women's subjection, their lack of dominion over their own lives, is the subtext of *Song of Solomon.* Milkman's great-grandmother Ryna dies of grief when Solomon leaves her still enslaved and burdened with twenty-one children. The sobbing echo emanating from Ryna's Gulch accompanies the song of Solomon, and it is part of Milk-man's education to listen to its anguished sound. When Milkman, full of his own self-importance, returns from the South eager to tell Pilate what she does not know, Pilate knocks him on the head; her granddaughter Hagar, the woman whose love Milkman took as he needed and then discarded, was dead. Lying "on the cool damp floor of the cellar," Milkman has another burst of awareness: "While he dreamt of flying, Hagar was dying. Sweet's silvery voice came back to him: 'Who'd he leave behind?' He [Solomon] left Ryna behind and twenty children. Twenty-one, since he dropped the one he tried to take with him. And Ryna had thrown herself all over the ground, lost her mind, and was still crying in a ditch. Who looked after those twenty-one children?" (336). Sorrow links the generations from Ryna to Hagar. In commemorating the details of Solomon's departure, the children of Shalimar also commemorate the aban-doned woman's appeal:

O Solomon don't leave me here
Cotton balls to choke me
O Solomon don't leave me here
Buckra's arms to yoke me . . . (307)

Thus, Morrison offers a critique of the flying African myth even as she inscribes it. Escape routes are not the same as routes to liberty. The entire novel is about the interdependence of individuals and the insurance of mutual life; redemp-tion cannot be individual. Pilate prevents Milkman from seeking flight from his responsibilities, from perpetuating the history of neglect. Milkman eventually learns to sympathize with the painful conditions of the women he is related to: that of being left behind (Ryna), mistreated (Ruth), controlled (his sisters), and devalued (Hagar).

Pilate's fidelity to the past does not promote an unquestioning acceptance of cultural tradition; the legacy of the past must be understood and reevaluated. It is significant that, North or South, Pilate moved "just barely within the boundaries of the elaborately socialized world of black people" (150). Because the community would not accept her lack of a navel, she becomes properly eccentric—she becomes who she is partly because she is an outsider who "threw away every assumption she had learned and began at zero." Because she is able to think for herself and examine her own values—"What do I need to know to stay alive? What is true in the world?"—she is able to realize her own creative power and experience a freedom of the spirit (148). Robert James Butler notes that Pilate is "one of the very few women in American literature capable of leading the picaresque life which is given so easily to the male protagonists of our literary traditions."[17] Yes, but picaresque with a difference. Milkman realizes that in contrast to his flying male ancestor, his aunt could fly "without ever leaving the ground" (340). Focusing on fathers and sons, the novel offers a different evaluation of the individualist, self-reliant model of male heroism celebrated in American society. Relying on a number of women, Milkman does not achieve selfhood on his own—he is coached by Pilate, loved by Ruth and Hagar, cared for by his sisters, guided by Circe, and healed by Sweet. This realization of indebtedness enables Milkman to fly in a liberatory mode.

A transformed Milkman Dead is able to affirm what Robert Smith, the insurance agent, could not: mutual life itself. Functioning true to his name, he becomes life's sustenance issuing from a maternal source. In the allegorical tableau with which the novel closes, Pilate is dying from the wound inflicted by Guitar; Milkman is inheriting her song and returning to the blues matrix into which he seeks to welcome Guitar with open arms. With the "blood oozing from her neck into his cupped hand," in the "darkness staining his hand," Milkman is baptized in the historical matrix of blackness; Pilate's burial mound is the womb out of which he springs towards Guitar saying, "Here I am" (340).

17. Robert James Butler, "Open Movement and Selfhood in Toni Morrison's *Song of Solomon*," *Centennial Review*, XXVIII–XXIX (1984–85), 75.

Unlike his father who takes from others and never gives, the son has a life to give to his alienated brother Guitar:

"You want me? Huh? You want my life?"
Life life life life.
. . . "You want my life?" Milkman was not shouting now. "You need it? Here." Without wiping away the tears, taking a deep breath, or even bending his knees—he leaped. As fleet and bright as a lodestar he wheeled toward Guitar and it did not matter which one of them would give up his ghost in the killing arms of his brother. (341)

That we are meant to go beyond the deadlock of the "killing arms" is surely indicated by the next and last sentence of the novel: "For now he knew what Shalimar knew: If you surrendered to the air, you could *ride* it." The stress on the word *knew* underscores the relationship between historical knowledge and freedom that the novel has established. Historically, the onus of understanding Guitar and of reaching out to him in succor rests upon Milkman, the middle-class protagonist whose father turned Guitar and his grandmother out on the street. Milkman is redeeming both his father and himself in this flying leap. The change envisioned comes from the top—physically, Milkman must leap down to meet Guitar. Perhaps it is to this ideal vision of a black fraternity based on love and service, united and secured in the knowledge of their history, that *Song of Solomon* is dedicated: "The fathers may soar / And the children may know their names."

Structurally the novel's end parallels the flying at the novel's beginning, though the two flights are diametrically opposed, the difference between them being the difference between despair and courage. Milkman's flight is reflective of spontaneous generosity arising from self-mastery. From his point of view, it did not matter that he might die; unmindful of his own security, he acts from a deeper source, a steady inner compass "bright as a lodestar." Here, the theme of the biblical Song of Solomon, "love is strong as death," merges with the African American motif of flight, redefined as engagement rather than escape.

The title of this family saga of three generations is a variant name of the biblical text called the Song of Songs. The allusion to the Bible signifies the historical appropriation of it in slave songs' liberation theology. African American spirituals are historic songs of "protest and defiance, based on the passion and eventual triumphs of the Hebrew slaves of Egypt." As James Cone observes,

"We are told that the people of Israel could not sing the Lord's song in a strange land. But, for Blacks, their *being* depended upon a song." Morrison's blues song of Solomon comes out of a "blues-spiritual matrix" shaped by "men and women of large vision and even larger voices."[18] Pilate's "powerful contralto" and Morrison's resonant, evocative prose with its biblical cadence keep this tradition alive.

The biblical Song of Songs belongs to an oral folk tradition, and according to Marcia Falk, who has translated the text from Hebrew into English, Solomon is not the speaker of these lyrics; as Falk suggests, he is more the king used for poetic contrast.[19] It is the wisdom of the biblical statement "love is strong as death" that is favorably contrasted to the famed wealth of Solomon, the king associated both with material wealth and the figurative wealth of wisdom. Morrison exploits both these aspects of Solomon and creatively adapts the third feature attributed to this famed king: a knowledge of the language of birds. This avian knowledge blends with the legend of African ancestors, giving Morrison a cluster of motifs with which to work. The spiritual wisdom and material wealth attributed to Solomon are divided between Pilate and Macon Dead, grandchildren of the flying slave ancestor Solomon. In the biblical songs celebrating sensuous love, the lovelorn speaker of many verses is a rural black woman looking for her lover in the city or beckoning him to her mother's vineyard/house, a woman whose beauty kindles the hostility of the city women. Her assertion of her blackness and conviction in her own beauty ("I am black and comely") contrasts with Morrison's young black woman, Hagar, who sadly lacks this self-esteem and in fact dies thinking she is ugly and unlovable, consumed by the capitalist market that sells good looks and a manufactured persona to women. Nonetheless, Pilate's vineyard becomes the site of love and life, countering the negativity of the Dead household in which sisters Corinthians and Lena spend their lives making artificial roses. Among other things, it is love that Pilate teaches Milkman; herself embodying what Paul Tillich has called *creative eros*, she offers a corrective to the various kinds of narrow or misguided identifications professed by Hagar, Ruth, Guitar, and Milkman.

18. Lerone Bennett, Jr., *Before the Mayflower: A History of Black America* (New York, 1984), 103; James Cone, qtd. in Angela Davis, "Black Women and Music," in *Wild Women in the Whirlwind*, 8; Bennett, *Before the Mayflower*, 103.

19. Marcia Falk, *Love Lyrics from the Bible: A Translation and Literary Study of the Song of Songs* (Sheffield, Eng., 1982), 134.

Morrison's novel recalls another work alluding to Solomon and the birds, *Concourse of the Birds*, the work of a twelfth-century Persian Sufi poet, Farid al-Din Attar. The hoopoe, an ambassador sent by Solomon to the Queen of Sheba, is the pilot who leads the birds to wisdom; his advice to each bird is to "release from thee whatever thou hast, one by one" in order to "become a lover . . . worthy of annihilation."[20] Such annihilation is not literal but refers instead to the extinction of the egotistic self and to the accompanying expansion of one's identifications. It could be said that in the course of his journey, Milkman becomes such a lover. For it is with the magnanimity of a lover that Milkman offers the gift of his life to Guitar: "You need it? Here" (341). This is an example of the weak Messianic power that an integrated knowledge of the past gives Milkman.

Inasmuch as Morrison's approach to the past in *Song of Solomon* can be read as an attempt to revise contemporary fragmentation with a narrative of continuity, it can also be charged with simplifying the problems of modernity. However, if this novel brackets the present in its attempt to construct a usable past and shape an identity that is both responsive and responsible to the past, Morrison's next novel, *Tar Baby*, problematizes the present, only gesturing to the liberation code of the past, a code set apart in legend and rendered inaccessible or inert in the postmodern present of advanced capitalism. *Tar Baby* revises the optimism of *Song of Solomon* by depicting the impasse of the present. However, this revision serves to bring out with increasing urgency the historian in Morrison. Her subsequent two novels, *Beloved* and *Jazz*, go further into the past, the objective being recovery: recovering that from which the present has still not recovered.

If Morrison may be charged with anything in relation to the past, especially in *Song of Solomon*, it is *piety*, Michael Roth's excellent term for what he identifies as "the third fundamental dimension of historical work." The other "two fundamental dimensions of historical investigation and representation" being "the empirical and the pragmatic. The former is the effort to 'get the past right,' to provide an interpretation of something in the past that is recognized as of that thing. The latter is the effort to find or create a usable past, something that can

---

20. Farid al-Din Attar, *Mantiq-al-Tayr (Concourse of the Birds)*, qtd. in Seyyed Hossein Nasr, *Islamic Art and Spirituality* (Albany, N.Y., 1987), 108.

be put in the service of a particular goal." As Roth observes, "no complex representation of the past is possible without both components":

[Piety] is not reducible to either the empirical or the pragmatic. Piety is the turning of oneself so as to be in relation to the past, to experience oneself as coming after (perhaps emerging out of or against) the past. This is the attempt at fidelity to (not correspondence with) the past. . . . When the dimension of piety is powerful in our historical work, we encounter the past by acknowledging its absence, its having been. . . . Through the dimension of piety . . . we acknowledge the claim that that thing has on us. The object that we acknowledge in this way is certainly *for us*, but piety is our refusal simply to *use* the object or to forget it . . . The dimension of piety reminds us of why we turn to (and stay with) the past at all.

It is not nostalgia but piety that informs Toni Morrison's return to the past—such a return is not a flight from the present but an acknowledgement of the "secret agreement between past generations and the present one," the claim of the past to its deliverance in and by the present.[21] If the agreement is also a secret or unconscious one, Morrison's piety is the attempt to disclose the secret, to make the unconscious conscious in the present. It is to give a conscience to the present, to make for it a guiding lodestar.

21. Roth, *The Ironist's Cage*, 16–17; Benjamin, *Illuminations*, 256.

4

PROSPERO'S SPELL AND THE QUESTION OF RESISTANCE: *Tar Baby*

And neither world thought the other world's thought, save
with a vague unrest.
——W. E. B. Du Bois, *The Souls of Black Folk*

Ninety-five per cent of my people poor
ninety-five per cent of my people black
ninety-five per cent of my people dead
you have heard it all before O Leviticus O Jeremiah
   O Jean-Paul Sartre

and now I see that these modern palaces have grown
out of the soil, out of the bad habits of their crippled owners
the Chrysler stirs but does not produce cotton
the Jupiter purrs but does not produce bread

out of the living stone, out of the living bone
of coral, these dead
towers; out of the coney
islands of our mind-

less architects, this death
of sons, of songs, of sunshine;
out of this dearth of coo ru coos, home-
less pigeons, this perturbation that does not signal health.
       ——Edward Brathwaite, "Caliban"

Juxtaposing the provincial with the metropolitan and charting various ge-
ographies of class, *Tar Baby* depicts the struggle over cultural definitions and
identifications in a postmodern world. In *Tar Baby*, Morrison allows the reader

to see the African American crisis of identity and alignment in colonial and postcolonial terms. Located between the two metropolitan capitals of New York and Paris in the French Caribbean, controlled by American and French capital and built by Haitian labor, the small island of Isle de Chevaliers serves as the setting for the characters' diasporic departures and arrivals. "The tale of the diaspora," according to Michael Hanchard, "holds a subversive resonance when contrasted with that of the nation-state. . . . It suggests a transnational dimension to black identity, for if the notion of an African diaspora is anything it is a human necklace strung together by a thread known as the slave trade."[1] Though Morrison activates this subversive dimension of the setting, it is important to note that *Tar Baby* is not so much about the Caribbean as it is about the contemporary dilemmas of African Americans. It is about Jadine Childs and Son Green's relations with each other, their positioning vis-à-vis Eloe, Florida, and New York City—the black South and black North—and their relations with the dominant culture and its institutions. African Americans must negotiate a place for themselves within a dominant culture; how they situate themselves with respect to their own history and culture is a pervasive theme of Morrison's novels. White American Valerian Street's mansion—the master's house—becomes symbolic of the dominant socioeconomic and commodifying cultural space from which the black characters seek routes of escape. The novel, however, does not offer any viable routes; what it does offer is a troubled critique.

It is worth noting here that *Tar Baby* re-examines conflicts that have surfaced forcefully in the three previous novels. One can better appreciate what Morrison is attempting to do in this novel's contemporary setting if one recalls the first novel, *The Bluest Eye*, in which class hierarchies fissure race solidarity and weaken cultural identity. Just as *The Bluest Eye* draws black characters of both genders from disparate classes (and shades) and situates them in one master narrative, a diverse class of black characters are brought together under the master's house in *Tar Baby*'s French Caribbean. The strategy of both novels is to unify the characters in their conflicting allegiances by grounding them in a dominant text. *The Bluest Eye* does so metaphorically by employing the Dick-and-Jane text; *Tar Baby* does so by situating the black characters in the white master's house. Pecola Breedlove's failure to achieve selfhood in 1941 gives

1. Michael Hanchard, "Identity, Meaning, and the African American," *Social Text*, XXIV (1990), 40.

way four decades later to Jadine's apparent success; however, on deeper analysis, the two women are merely different sides of the same coin. Pecola is convinced she is ugly because evidence is everywhere; on billboards, in the eyes of black and white adults, within the home and outside it. Jadine has no doubt she is beautiful because the evidence lies in the cover of *Elle* flaunting her face. But Jadine is no more self-defined than Pecola. As a fashion model she has subscribed to an aesthetics of commodification; as a student of art history, she has become properly Eurocentric. She tells Valerian, "Picasso *is* better than an Itumba mask. The fact that he was intrigued by them is proof of *his* genius, not the mask-maker's" (74). Here Jadine Childs is the native in whom the hegemonic project of colonization is complete.

The novel invests little sympathy for Jadine's predicament. In *Song of Solomon*, middle-class Milkman Dead's salvation lies in returning to his origins and integrating a subaltern consciousness; but Jadine, his female counterpart in *Tar Baby*, has no means of getting back to her origins—this culturally orphaned, Sorbonne-educated model has no moorings in the ancestral traditions of resistance and no cultural guides to pilot her consciousness. As a woman, Jadine has less incentive than a character like Milkman Dead to go back to her roots—what she finds are pie women and fertility women. The sought-after "ancient properties" come to have a disturbingly essentialist female character, their signifiers being Thérèse's milk-giving breasts and the African woman's proudly held eggs. Recall Sula's poignant reply to Eva's command that she get married and have babies: "I don't want to make somebody else. I want to make myself." In *Tar Baby*, the upwardly mobile Jadine is damned for the same impulse. Sula's desire to make herself receives authorial sympathy while Jadine's individualism appears contemptible. The difference between Sula and Jadine is that the latter is a postintegration, postmodern character carrying the privileges of assimilation along with its bourgeois ills. For all her iconoclasm, Sula is not rebelling against her blackness but protesting the oppression of black women within the culture. Educated and privileged, Jadine both dissociates herself from her blackness and commodifies it in the fashion worlds of New York and Paris. *Tar Baby* grounds Jadine's apostasy in a historical trajectory of colonization and class mobility by assimilation. Characters like Jadine earn the animus of their creator because they have power to affect, for better or worse, the lives of others—especially those others of the collectivity with whom they deny affiliation—but in them, the historical narrative of black liberation seems to founder in the capitalist ethic of individualism.

Morrison's comments during a 1981 interview are illuminating: "This civilization of black people, which was underneath the white civilization, was there with its own everything. Everything of that civilization was not worth hanging on to, but some of it was, and nothing has taken its place while it is being dismantled. There is a new, capitalistic, modern American black which is what everybody thought was the ultimate in integration. To produce Jadine, that's what it was for. I think there is some danger in the result of that production. It cannot replace certain essentials from the past."[2] Morrison provides more sympathy for Son, the peasant or briar-patch rabbit who gets caught in between two worlds. Enamored by Jadine, he cannot be part of her world, but neither can he remain in his; we leave him practically marooned on the island. The novel attempts to invest Son's cultural dislocation with meaning from the mythic past, with the emancipatory meaning of the word *maroon*. (The OED gives as its first definition, "one of a class of negros, originally fugitive slaves, living in the mountains and forests of Dutch Guiana and the West Indies.") At the same time, Morrison also exposes via Jadine the sexism of a subaltern black man such as Son. These competing claims of racial, class, and gender identity make *Tar Baby* a troubled and troubling novel, even as its explosive text of race relations ensured its author the cover of *Newsweek*.

The reason for this commercial success appears to be its provocative Manichean theme. Jean Strouse wrote in that *Newsweek* cover story: "In the new novel, *Tar Baby*, Morrison takes on a much larger world than she has before, drawing a composite picture of America in black and white." Nellie McKay accounts for the greater popularity of *Song of Solomon* and *Tar Baby* by suggesting that these novels "are considerably less confusing, threatening, or intimidating for white readers than the earlier books." She also explains that "their 'black texts' were often unrecognized."[3] Indeed, if *Tar Baby*'s black text was recognized, the romantic affair/battle of wits between a jet-setting fashion model and a Rastafarian-looking black man would be much more perturbing; the banter-filled dialogue between the white master and his black butler would cease to be an entertaining spectacle. Linking several narratives of bondage and insurgency—the tar baby folk tale, the maroon story of slave insurrection,

2. Toni Morrison, interview with Charles Ruas, 1981, in *Conversations*, 105.

3. Jean Strouse, "Toni Morrison's Black Magic," *Newsweek*, March 30, 1981, p. 52; Nellie McKay, Introduction to *Critical Essays on Toni Morrison*, ed. McKay (Boston, 1988), 6.

and Shakespeare's *Tempest*—*Tar Baby* stages a contemporary parable of alienation and resistance to economic and cultural imperialism.

Bringing Afro-Caribbean and Afro-American characters together under the master's roof, the novel activates the oppressive history that brought them there by recreating the dramatic conflicts of *The Tempest*. Parallels between Shakespeare's island ruled by Prospero and the Caribbean islands colonized by West European powers are readily apparent. *The Tempest* has been read and performed as the prototype of a colonialist narrative; Sylvan Barnet cited as an example of this interpretation Jonathan Miller's 1970 production of the play in London, in which Caliban appears as a black, uneducated field hand, Ariel as a black house slave, and Prospero as the exploiting slave owner. In *The Pleasures of Exile*, West Indian writer George Lamming explored these *Tempest* relationships: "If Prospero could be seen as the symbol of the European imperial enterprise, then Caliban should be embraced as the continuing possibility of a profound revolutionary change initiated by Touissant L'Ouverture in the Haitian war of independence."[4] Morrison's imaginary island off Dominique is named Isle de Chevaliers after the island's founding revolutionaries, the African slaves who slipped their French yoke three hundred years before. Representing different class interests, the various characters in *Tar Baby* play out the tensions between Prospero, Ariel, and Caliban and the attendant themes of power, betrayal, and resistance. In a complication of the *Tempest* plot, Morrison has Son (Caliban) fall in love with the Sorbonne-educated, mulatta Jadine, who in her role as Miranda is more Valerian's daughter than her foster-father/uncle Sydney's.

In the Caribbean, Valerian Street, the white American industrialist known as "the Candy King," lives the life of an exile as does Shakespeare's magician Prospero; like the latter's, Valerian's control over his domain seems absolute. He buys the island for himself as a refuge in his retirement from the candy business; "over the years he sold off parts of it," inaugurating the erosion of life on the island.[5] The economic exploitation of the island's resources and its

4. See O. Mannoni, *Prospero and Caliban: The Psychology of Colonization*, trans. Pamela Powesland (New York, 1964); Sylvan Barnet, "The Tempest on the Stage," in *The Tempest*, ed. Barnet (New York, 1987), 224; George Lamming, Introduction to *The Pleasures of Exile* (London, 1984), 6.

5. Toni Morrison, *Tar Baby* (New York, 1981), 53. Subsequent page references will be cited within parentheses in the text.

people, the social and cultural displacement of the local folk, is articulated allegorically by the disastrous changes in the natural landscape, the flora and fauna and seasons:

The men had already folded the earth where there had been no fold and hollowed her where there had been no hollow, which explains what happened to the river. It crested, then lost its course, and finally its head. Evicted from the place where it had lived, and forced into unknown turf, it could not form its pools and waterfalls, and ran every which way. The clouds gathered together, stood still and watched the river scuttle around the forest floor, crash headlong into the haunches of hills with no notion of where it was going, until exhausted, ill and grieving, it slowed to a stop just twenty leagues short of the sea.

The clouds looked at each other, then broke apart in confusion. Fish heard their hooves as they raced off to carry the news of the scatterbrained river to the peaks of hills and the tops of the champion daisy trees. But it was too late. (9–10)

Critics have expressed their dislike of the personification of nature: John Irving finds it excessive, Pearl K. Buck resents the "incessant anthropomorphizing of nature," and according to Richard Falk, the use of pathetic fallacy burdens the prose. However, this personification is meaningful if we see it as an extension of the Caliban theme. As George Lamming notes, "Caliban himself like the island he inherited is at once a landscape and a human situation." Along with the erosion of land—and of a people's relation to it—occurs the erosion of a world view, a way of inhabiting the universe. The stripping of the rain forest begun by the prosperous Valerian invokes Prospero's speech in which he recounts the deeds of the "rough magic" by which he dominated the "elves of hills, brooks, standing lakes, and groves" of the isle:

. . . I have bedimmed
The noontide sun, called forth the mutinous winds,
And 'twixt the green sea and the azure vault
Set roaring war . . .
. . . the strong-based promontory
Have I made shake and by the spurs plucked up
The pine and cedar. . . .

In *Tar Baby*, ecological damage is the visible counterpart of cultural displacement, both long-term effects of colonization. The landscape ravaged by the
dictates of capitalism becomes a metaphor of cultural rootlessness in a novel
whose characters are displaced or in exile of one kind or another: Valerian and
his wife Margaret, their son Michael, the servants Sydney and Ondine, Jadine
and Son—all are unsettled beings. In *Tar Baby*, the landscape's own story of
colonization and subjection establishes a moral and political ground from which
to assess the actions of the characters on the island. One thinks of Edward
Brathwaite's poems, which make a similar moral appeal. In the poem "Hex" in
Mother Poem, a collection about the poet's homeland in Barbados, Brathwaite
personifies Barbados as "black sycorax my mother" with "a white trail of salt
. . . upon her cheek," for "all have dealt treacherously with her": "all the peaks,
the promontories, the coves, the glitter / bays of her body have been turned
into money / the grass ploughed up and fed into mortar of houses / for master
for mister for massa for mortal baas."[6]

On top of a hill, on this land of the diminished rain forest, sits the symbol
of metropolitan control: Valerian's mansion, L'Arbe de la Croix. In this natural
paradise, his greenhouse is "a place of controlled ever-flowering life to greet
death in" (53). Instead of the natural exuberant life of the tropics, Valerian as
demigod imposes his own airless greenhouse with the characteristic disregard
of the colonizer for existing rhythms and patterns of life in the colony. The
cross (Croix) is an appropriate symbol of colonial intrusion into the garden
(Arbe), since natives' conversion to Christianity marked the colonial variant
of the postlapsarian divided self.

Like Caliban's isle in Shakespeare, the Isle de Chevaliers is full of sounds
and presences, not all of which are restful. Roaming the island in freedom are
the ancient slaves: black, blind, and riding naked on horseback, their mythic
presence haunts the island and supplements the range of black subjects and
histories assembled. Though eclipsed, black oppositional sentiment is projected
and preserved in this mythic presence. The American Valerian abides by the

6. John Irving, "Morrison's Black Fable," *New York Times Book Review* March 29, 1981, pp.
1, 30–31; Pearl K. Buck, "Self-Seekers," *Commentary*, LXXII (August, 1981), 56–60; Richard Falk,
"Fables For Our Times: Six Novels," *Yale Review*, LXXI (1982), 254*ff*.; Lamming, *The Pleasures of
Exile*, 118; William Shakespeare, *The Tempest*, ed. Sylvan Barnet (New York, 1987), 33–48; Edward
Brathwaite, "Hex," *Mother Poem* (Oxford, Eng., 1977), 45–47.

colonial French version of the island's legend/history: "one hundred French chevaliers were roaming the hills on horses. Their swords were in their scabbards and their epaulets glittered in the sun. Backs straight, shoulders high— alert but restful in the security of the Napoleonic Code." For Son, on the other hand, "one hundred black men on one hundred unshod horses rode blind and naked through the hills and had done so for hundreds of years. They knew the rain forest when it was a rain forest, they knew where the river began, where the roots twisted above the ground" (206). Frantz Fanon's words come to mind: "Decolonization is the meeting of two forces, opposed to each other by their very nature."[7] The novel traces the contentions among the various characters, indexed in the novel's epigraph ("For it hath been declared unto me of you, my brethren . . . that there are contentions among you"), to their colonial origins.

Prospero rules over his servants, Ariel and Caliban, by creating in classic colonial style hierarchies of class—airy Ariel being superior to earthy, menial Caliban. The role of Ariel, who answers to Prospero's every beck and call, is shared by Sydney, the butler, and his wife Ondine, the cook. Like Ariel to Prospero, they have bonded themselves to Valerian, following him from Baltimore to Philadelphia to the Caribbean. The underclass is situated outside the house in the yard; they are the local blacks, Gideon and Thérèse, whose names are not considered worth knowing by their American superiors. Sydney and Ondine hail them by the generic names Yardman and Mary. They share the status of Caliban with the native son of the American South, Son (William Green), who is "among that great underclass of undocumented men," the "Huck Finns," "Nigger Jims," and "Calibans" (166). Sydney and Ondine disown any sense of connection with Son, who "wasn't a Negro—meaning one of them" (102). The haglike figure of Thérèse resembles Caliban's mother Sycorax, who, while physically absent in The Tempest, is marked as Prospero's adversary. This Sycorax figure comes to life in Thérèse when, in the last scene of Tar Baby, she has Caliban/Son choose between Jadine and the resisting slave ancestors. Just as the Tempest ends with Miranda's departure, leaving Caliban to regain the island for himself, Tar Baby ends with Jadine's departure, leaving Son roaming the island and the reader figuring the meaning of his predicament.

7. Frantz Fanon, Wretched of the Earth, trans. Constance Farrington (New York, 1965), 36.

*

As important as *The Tempest* to the novel's signifying system is the recurrent motif of the tar baby taken from black folklore. There are many variations of the tar baby story, only the basic outline of which is relevant to the novel: resourceful Brer Rabbit of the briar patch has a trap set for him by Brer Fox; the trap is an attractive figure of tar to which Brer Rabbit is meant to become stuck. In the folk tale, the fascinated Brer Rabbit does become entangled in the tar; the more he struggles the more he is stuck; he only escapes to his briar patch by wile. Son and Jadine are implicated in double roles as both snarer and ensnared. Although the narrative perspective shifts from Son as Brer Rabbit–Jadine as entrapper to Jadine as Brer Rabbit–Son as entrapper, the narrative viewpoint is less sympathetic to Jadine's entrapment. While Son has affiliations with the mythic swamp horsemen, Jadine refuses to affiliate herself with the swamp women, either the mythic beings of the island or real ones like Thérèse and Alma Estée working in Valerian's backyard and Son's relatives in Florida.

Son is himself a tar baby whose blackness confronts Jadine. We witness Son enter the sleeping Jadine's bedroom in an attempt "to breathe into her the smell of tar and its shining consistency before he crept away" (120). On her way home from a picnic trip, Jadine gets stuck in the swamp while Son is away getting gasoline for the jeep. Walking towards the mossy floor beneath the shade of trees, Jadine, sketch pad in hand, "sank up to her knees": "She dropped the pad and charcoal and grabbed the waist of a tree. . . . She struggled to lift her feet and sank an inch or two farther down into the moss-covered jelly. The pad with Son's face badly sketched looked up at her and the women hanging in the trees looked down at her. . . . The women looked down from the rafters of the trees and stopped murmuring. They were delighted when they first saw her, thinking a runaway child was restored to them. But upon looking closer they saw differently. This girl was fighting to get away from them" (182–83). Son's sketched image looking up from the swamp identifies him as the tar baby—Sydney identified Son, a native of Florida, as a "stinking, ignorant swampnigger" (100). Finding herself in the predicament of Brer Rabbit, Jadine struggles with tar, her blackness. This scene builds upon two earlier scenes in which we find her struggling with her racial identity. Structurally, the scene recalls when Jadine, preening in a fur coat sent her by a Parisian admirer, sees Son's black face confronting her in her bedroom mirror and "struggle[s] to pull herself from his image" (114). More thematically, it recalls Jadine's uncomfortable yet wistful encounter with an African woman, a stranger in a Parisian supermarket; the arrogance and "unphotographable beauty" of "that mother/ sister/she" clearly impresses Jadine, who carries her own blackness with ambivalence (46). Suddenly it is important for Jadine to be approved by this tar woman; however, on her way out the African woman spits in Jadine's direction, leaving her derailed. Jadine's fall in the swamp prefigures her trip with Son to Florida, where she feels smothered by the the women of Eloe. While Son is able to identify himself with the maleness represented by the horsemen, Jadine cannot identify with the swamp women, the female counterparts of the resisting ancestors.

Here *Tar Baby* revisits from another direction the conflict of nationalism and feminism raised in *Sula*. In *Sula*, the community was reproved for failing to appreciate a feminist position; in *Tar Baby*, Jadine is reproved for repudiating the counternationalist project of cultural resistance. Instead of sympathizing with Jadine's refusal of oppressive gender roles (as she perceives them among the women of Eloe), the novel valorizes the strength, the "exceptional female- ness" of peasant women's cultural traditions. Swamp and tar become metaphors for this strength: "The women hanging from the trees were . . . arrogant— mindful as they were of their value, their exceptional femaleness; knowing as they did that the first world of the world was built with their sacred properties; that they alone could hold together the stones of pyramids and the rushes of Moses's crib" (183). These women with "ancient properties," and those the novel is dedicated to, held the community together like tar and did not consider themselves weak. To Jadine, swamp and tar have properties that impede. She does not want "to settle for wifely competence when she could be almighty, to settle for fertility rather than originality, nurturing instead of building" (269). However, the novel levels this feminist point of view with Son's: "She kept barking at him about equality, sexual equality, as though he thought women were inferior. He couldn't understand that" (268). Using Son's point of view, Morrison informs the reader about the history of black women's struggle, one that the politics of liberal feminism does not engage: "[His ex-wife] Cheyenne was driving a beat-up old truck at age nine, four years before he could even shift gears, and she could drop a pheasant like an Indian. His mother's memory was kept alive by those who remembered how she roped horses when she was a girl. His grandmother built a whole cowshed with only Rosa to help. In fact the room Jadine has slept in, Rosa built herself which was why it didn't have any windows. Anybody who thought women were inferior didn't come out of north Florida" (268). These rural black women have no need for the gains of a liberal feminism, whose ideal of equality Jadine defends. The struggles of these black women have to do with poverty and physical hardship, a history Jadine cannot comprehend. In representing the chasms of class, Morrison questions Jadine's achievement of emancipation from the perspective of the women she defines herself against, for "underneath her efficiency and know-it-all sass" are delicate wind chimes: "Nine rectangles of crystal, rainbowed in the light. Fragile pieces of glass tinkling as long as the breeze was gentle" (220); her room appears "uncomfortable-looking" and fragile, "like a dollhouse for an absent doll" (131). What she *is* liberated from is responsibility to her aged aunt and uncle, her culture, her history, all of which is burdensome and restrictive to her. Jadine, who is happy "making it" in the city, urges Son, who is not "able to get excited about money," to "*get* able," "*get* excited" (171).

If Son is a tar-baby trap for Jadine, he is also Brer Rabbit, a black man who is caught in the white farmer/master's tar baby. Though Son's support for his own people has not been weakened by a hegemonic education, which he has resisted, he does succumb to Jadine's way of seeing things. However, Son also receives his share of authorial criticism for his provincial, nostalgic, and unrealistic outlook: his naive attitude toward money, his idealization of the black woman in her maternal role, and his romanticization of Eloe. He is hurt by Jadine's contemptuous view of his folk and their traditional black ways; her grimly realistic definition of the briar patch competes with Son's sentimental picture. She reveals as false consciousness Son's many assumptions about the wholesomeness of the agrarian past. There is nothing romantic about poverty, nothing autonomous about an all-black town run by white electricity, nothing enabling about not being educated or part of the institutions of modernity. Jadine delivers these hard critiques and must, in turn, hear from Son the scathing critique of postmodernity—there is nothing pretty about being objectified on the cover of a fashion magazine, nothing positive about conforming to the dehumanizing creed of high capitalism, nothing valuable in being educated to forget where she came from, nothing humane about her relationship to her aunt and uncle, nothing inspiring in the aesthetics of consumption. This impasse between them is symptomatic of a larger crisis of the third world locked in the arms of the first.

Jadine's uncritical alignment of herself with Valerian's world is criticized in no uncertain terms. The mix of eros and the erosion of self that characterizes Son's relationship with Jadine is prefigured in the image of Jadine's nude figure lying on the black coat made of the fur of ninety baby seals. That Son is identified with an area that has ninety black houses in Eloe has chilling significance. Having accepted the death of ninety seals as the price for her self-indulgence, Jadine succeeds in making Son willing to accept his alienation from Eloe as the price of his future with her. Jadine has ceased to be a daughter and threatens to take away his identity as Son, "the name that called forth the true him," for the "other selves were . . . fabrications of the moment, misinformation required to protect Son from harm and to secure that one reality at least" (139). Looking at the photos Jadine had taken of his family and friends in Eloe, Son finds himself thinking "they all looked stupid, backwoodsy, dumb, dead. . . ." However, his next thought is, "I have to find her": "Whatever she wants, I have to do it, want it" (272–73). For Son, a vital identification—and along with it a way of being in the world—is being undermined, a stability eroded. He is stuck *and* lost. The difficulty Son as Brer Rabbit has in outsmarting the fox is the crisis in Morrison's adaptation of the folk tale. The triumphant ending of the tar baby tale creates a tension: although Son cannot see a way out, the tale impresses upon the reader the need for freedom from this contemporary state of bondage.

In order to better understand Morrison's indictment of Jadine, it is necessary to go back a century and glance at black abolitionist and suffragist Frances Harper's *Iola Leroy*, a novel that attempted to articulate the meaning of emancipation for black women following Reconstruction. Iola is a woman of mixed descent, the daughter of a plantation owner who has grown up considering herself white. Forced into slavery then rescued by Union soldiers during the Civil War, Iola Leroy has the option of passing for white at the end of the war but chooses to ally herself with her race. This, at the time of Jim Crow segregation, is a significant act charged with idealism. The forging of an intellectual elite committed to the cause of the race is an important theme in Harper's novel. Education is presented as a good investment, enabling assimilating blacks to uplift their race. A century later, *Tar Baby*, whose black woman protagonist is the antithesis of Iola, presents the bitter fruits of assimilation: an ignorance of black history, an alienated and alienating sense of individualism, and the breakdown of any notion of responsibility. Education does not allow a politics of return to the people, producing instead an educated alienation from the working class.

Both Toni Morrison and Alice Walker are severe on the educated black woman who fastens her metropolitan gaze on the culture from which she came. Alice Walker's story "Everyday Use" is an insightful portrayal of an ideological chasm generated by a displacement of class and culture through education. A young woman named Dee, enabled by her family and community to go to college, becomes the "cultured" one, set apart from both her "backward" sister and her mother, who feel Dee has them "sitting trapped and ignorant underneath her voice."[8] With a consciousness fashioned by the dominant class, Dee takes snapshots of her family's picturesque poverty to show her college friends. The eye of her camera, like Jadine's eye, freezes people in its alienating frame. That such a gaze comes from one of their own is an outrage to Walker and Morrison; it is a danger endemic to the very process of education.

Both Walker and Morrison would endorse Son's criticism of Jadine's education: "The truth is whatever you learned in those colleges that didn't include me ain't shit. What did they teach you about me? What tests did they give? . . . And you don't know anything, anything at all about your children and anything at all about your mama and your papa. You find out about me, you educated nitwit!" (264–65). Jadine thinks she is indebted to Valerian for educating her, but, as Son reminds her, it is her aunt and uncle who secured her privileges with their lifetime's labor, securing her "everything. Europe. The future. The world" (26). Sydney and Ondine, of course, have not bargained for her alienation from them. The extent of Jadine's incomprehension of her aunt's needs is made evident in the Christmas present she buys for her, "a stunning black chiffon dress," and "shoes with zircons studding the heels" (90). She has no idea that her aunt's feet are swollen with pain from a lifetime of standing too long in the kitchen. It is also deeply ironic that Sydney does not claim any kinship with Jadine while he serves her at the table; the laws of class decorum appear to be stronger than the ties of kinship. Sydney "was perfect at those dinners when his niece sat down with his employers, as perfect as he was when he served Mr. Street's friends" (74): "He kept his eyes on the platter, or the table setting, or his feet, or the hands of those he was serving, and never made eye contact with any of them, including his niece" (62). Even when the subject of conversation is Sydney, we are told that "Jadine did not look at her uncle" (75). This charade soon becomes reality; Jadine disowns any responsibility to

8. Alice Walker, "Everyday Use," in In Love and Trouble (New York, 1973), 50.

Sydney and Ondine, leaving them as she leaves Son for upper-class Parisian society.

The poignancy of Ondine and Sydney's situation vis-à-vis their niece is undercut by their own perpetuation of class hierarchies. The reader is meant to share the "disappointment nudging contempt" that Valerian feels at his household's response to Son's intrusion, "for the outrage Jade and Sydney and Ondine exhibited in defending property and personnel that did not belong to them from a black man who was one of their own" (145). Morrison is as sardonic about Margaret Street's fear of the black-man-as-rapist as she is about Sydney's presumed superiority over Son. Margaret refers to Son as a "gorilla"; Sydney tells Son, "If this was my house, you would have a bullet in your head. . . . You can tell it's not my house because you are still standing upright" (162). The reader is meant to note the bigotry that Sydney displays in differentiating his class from Son's: "I am a Phil-a-delphia Negro mentioned in the book of the very same name. My people owned drugstores and taught school while yours were still cutting their faces open so as to be able to tell one from the other" (163). To maintain his class affiliation, Sydney refuses to communicate with Son and calls Gideon "Yardman" lest their familiarity or fraternity undermine his cultivated position of respectability.

We come away perturbed by Jadine's lone trajectory of success, which, viewed from the dominant ideology of individualism, should seem laudable and appropriate: in avoiding the "ghetto mentality," she succeeds in making a better life for herself and is able to make choices that ensure her freedom as a woman. But Morrison's critique of this black daughter is unmistakable. For all practical purposes, the role and function of Jadine's education has been to dissolve her debts to her family and culture by taking her out of their orbit. Lerone Bennett, Jr., frames the issue starkly: betrayal is the historic role of the middle class; grown out of the very pores of oppression, it also by its very position abdicates responsibility to an ongoing struggle. This is also the point that Frantz Fanon makes about the educated middle class of postcolonial nations; he appreciates the fact that such an educated class, fostered by the colonial apparatus of power and subjection, is fated to become the tool of capitalism. For Fanon, revolutionary pedagogy lies in the middle class "betray[ing] the calling fate has marked out for it, and put[ting] itself at school with the people." However, he observes "unhappily" that such a revolutionary trajectory is seldom seen: "rather, [the middle class] disappears with its soul set at peace into the shocking ways . . . of a traditional bourgeoisie, of a bourgeoisie which is stupidly, contemptibly, cynically bourgeois."⁹

To articulate the past historically does not mean to recognize it "the way it really was." It means to seize hold of a memory as it flashes up at a moment of danger. . . . The danger affects both the content of the tradition and its receivers. The same threat hangs over both: that of becoming a tool of the ruling classes. In every era an attempt must be made anew to wrest tradition away from a conformism that is about to overpower it.

—Walter Benjamin, "Theses on the Philosophy of History"

By situating the narrative about Jadine's cultural displacement through education—and through her, Son's displacement—in a neocolonial field and framing it with the legend of a slave insurrection, Morrison accentuates the historical roots of this predicament and registers the need for a contemporary challenge to it. *Tar Baby* shares with other postcolonial literature what is an abiding concern: "disidentifying whole societies from the sovereign codes of cultural organization, and an inherently dialectical intervention in the hegemonic production of cultural meaning."¹⁰ The impasse generated by Son's encounter with Jadine is a historically charged stalemate pointing to the ways in which education and assimilation have served the race-class structures of society without ushering progressive changes.

In *Tar Baby*, the reader is left holding the tension of Son's predicament, one that marks the contemporary moment. The final question of choice posed to Son on the personal level—whether or not to follow Jadine—is meant to reverberate as a larger political crisis. Clearly, the problem—identified by Brathwaite as "this perturbation that does not signal health"—is much wider, pertaining to the neocolonial organization of the economy and hegemonic reproduction of the culture of capitalism. When Thérèse asks Son to choose, the two options are cultural erosion (Jadine's lifestyle) or resistance (the blind horsemen's response). "Forget her [Jadine]," Thérèse advises Son. "There is nothing in her parts for you. She has forgotten her ancient properties. . . . Choose them [the blind horsemen]" (305–306). "Are you sure?" are Son's last

9. Lerone Bennett, Jr., "The Betrayal of the Betrayal: The Crisis of the Black Middle Class," *The Challenge of Blackness* (Chicago, 1972), 57; Fanon, *Wretched of the Earth*, 150.

10. Stephen Slemon, "Monuments of Empire: Allegory/Counter-Discourse/Post-Colonial Writing," *Kunapipi*, IX (1987), 14.

words. It is also the question the reader may well ask. Observe, following Benjamin, how the narrative seizes a memory as it flashes up at a moment of danger, a danger that affects both the content of the slave tradition of resistance and its receivers. Thérèse is essentially warning Son against "becoming a tool of the ruling classes."[11]

The concluding scene of the novel is metaphorical. Son's gradual move from crawling over rocks to standing, walking, and eventually running imply an evolutionary movement. The novel suggests Son's identification with the blind horsemen as "he threw out his hands to guide and steady his going." That he is engaged in a salutory process is evident by the assistance he gets from the natural environment: "By and by he walked steadier, now steadier. The mist lifted and the trees stepped back a bit as if to make the way easier for a certain kind of man. Then he ran. Lickety-split. Lickety-split" (306). Thus, the ending merges Brer Rabbit's escape from Brer Fox's trap with the blind horsemen's escape from bondage. W. E. B. Du Bois' brooding short story "The Coming of John," from which comes the first epigraph to this chapter, makes an interesting comparison. It charts the displacement by education of a native son, John, from his own people. It ends with the figure of "a black man hurrying on with an ache in his heart, seeing neither sun nor sea," while "thundering towards him" is the "noise of horses galloping, galloping on."[12] Son's story also recapitulates the emancipation narrative of the slaves: if the novel's beginning suggests the escape of a fugitive jumping ship, the ending clearly encourages an identification of Son with the fugitive horsemen. The novel suggests that Son's route to freedom is one that requires an engagement with the liberation narrative of the past.

As at the end of *Song of Solomon*, what we are left with at the end of *Tar Baby* is a highly suggestive image. Just as Milkman Dead's flying leap is a metaphor for his emergent consciousness, Son's running lickety-split on the terrain of the blind horsemen may be read as a metaphor of pre-emergence, of a nascent form of cultural resistance. Even though the reclamation at the end of the novel remains a metaphoric one, the conclusion effects a disidentification with Prospero's ordering of the world, with what Stephen Slemon calls "the sovereign codes of cultural organization." Morrison leaves Son at what Nigerian writer Chinua Achebe has called the "crossroads of cultures," a postcolonial

---

11. Benjamin, *Illuminations*, 257.

12. Du Bois, *The Souls of Black Folk*, 262–63.

site that has, in his words, "a certain dangerous potency; dangerous because a man might perish there wrestling with multiple-headed spirits, but also he might be lucky and return to his people with the boon of prophetic vision."[13]

In terms of Morrison's literary trajectory, the novel seems to be leading inexorably to the exploration in Beloved of slavery, the point of unity where all the disparate segments of black life belong before they disperse. Both Song of Solomon and, to a lesser extent, Tar Baby take their male protagonists to the very edge of the present into an identification with a legendary past as a testimony of a burgeoning awareness. It is not surprising that in her fifth novel, Beloved, she sheds the present entirely to immerse her black characters in the matrix of history and to acquaint the modern reader with the ancient properties of black women. In Beloved, Morrison is able to say what Tar Baby has difficulty articulating from within the fragmentations of postmodernity: "For one lost all lost. The chain that held them would save all or none."[14]

13. Slemon, "Monuments of Empire"; Chinua Achebe, Morning Yet on Creation Day: Essays (Garden City, N.Y., 1975), 67.

14. Morrison, Beloved, 110.

5

ON THE ROCKING LOOM OF HISTORY,
A NET TO HOLD THE PAST:
Beloved

We could have told them a different story.
—Harriet Jacobs,
Incidents in the Life of a Slave Girl

Shuttles in the rocking loom of history,
the dark ships move, the dark ships move

. . . .

weave toward New World littorals that are
mirage and myth and actual shore.

Voyage through death,
               voyage whose chartings are unlove.
Voyage through death
          to life upon these shores.
—Robert Hayden, "Middle Passage"

W estern historiography struggles against fiction," wrote Michel de Certeau, which "narrates one thing in order to tell something else." He elaborates, fiction "is a witch whom knowledge must labor to hold and to identify through its exorcising. . . . It is only a drifting meaning. It is the siren from whom the historian must defend himself, like Ulysses tied to the mast." The novel *Beloved* embodies this witchery, this other knowledge, but Toni Morrison does a different kind of exorcising than Certeau's historian. Jean-Pierre Vernant's formulation of an alternative history aptly describes *Beloved* as a historical novel: "History as celebrated by Mnemosoune is a deciphering of the invisible, a geography of the supernatural. . . . It throws a bridge between the world of the living and that beyond to which everything that leaves the light of day must return." In exploring her characters' traumatic memories, something that is rarely done in objective and subjective (autobiographical) historical accounts of slavery, Morrison is finally, in William Andrews' phrase, "telling a free story."[1] The representation of slavery in *Beloved* is made powerful by the positioning of desire at center stage, precisely what had found only a choked articulation all through slavery and in the emancipation narratives that emerged from it. Morrison moves us into what Barbara Christian calls "the chaotic space of mother-love/mother-pain, daughter-love/daughter-pain."

The conflict at the center of *Beloved* gets to the heart of the trauma of slavery: Sethe is the slave mother who dares to claim her children as her own property instead of the slaveholder's. If the master could subject the slave children in bondage to a slow "social death," the mother could release them through physical death.[2] Infanticide, Sethe's raw act of defiance, runs counter to the slave community's response of resistance, namely, their determined effort to keep family ties *alive* despite the master's attempt to sunder them. As in other novels by Morrison, the relationship between the individual and community is a conflictual one that allows her to probe the key nodes of tension within the social group. Sethe, the central protagonist of *Beloved*, incurs rancor and resentment from the women in the community because of her refusal to define herself as a breeder of slaves. In the course of the novel, Morrison redirects this moral outrage to the institution of slavery. As Andrew Levy notes, "unspeakability" is the challenge Morrison works with, "because the institutionalized parameters of guilt and responsibility do not provide the vocabulary to 'tell,' legally or narratively, the anomalies of a slave mother's infanticide." The traumatic nature of that experience is voiced in the nonfigurative meaning

---

1. Michel de Certeau, *Heterologies: Discourse on the Other*, trans. Brian Massumi (Minneapolis, Minn., 1986), 200, 202; Jean-Pierre Vernant, qtd. in Michael M. J. Fischer, "Ethnicity and the Post-Modern Arts of Memory," in *Anthropology as Cultural Critique: An Experimental Moment in the Human Sciences*, ed. George E. Marcus and Michael M. J. Fischer (Chicago, 1986), 194; William L. Andrews, *To Tell a Free Story: The First Century of Afro-American Autobiography, 1760–1865* (Urbana, Ill., 1986); Barbara Christian, "'Somebody Forgot to Tell Somebody Something': African-American Women's Historical Novels," in *Wild Women in the Whirlwind*, 339.

2. The concept of social death is developed in Orlando Patterson's *Slavery and Social Death* (Cambridge, Mass., 1982). I am indebted to Abdul JanMohamed for pointing out the theme of social death in *Beloved*.

of possession. As Cathy Caruth emphasizes, "To be traumatized is precisely to be possessed by an image or event." Trauma, as the figure of Beloved uncannily registers, is "the literal return of the event against the will of the one it inhabits." According to Caruth, "It is this literality and its insistent return which thus constitutes trauma and points towards its enigmatic core: the delay or incompletion in knowing, or even in seeing, an overwhelming occurrence that then remains, in its return, absolutely *true* to the event. It is indeed this truth of traumatic experience that forms the center of its pathology or its symptoms; it is not a pathology, that is, of falsehood or displacement of meaning, but of history itself."[3]

The seeds of the novel were planted back in the 1970s when Toni Morrison undertook the editing of *The Black Book,* a collection of "original raw material documenting our [black] life"; in the process she discovered many painful incidents of black history, including the infamous story of Margaret Garner. She cites an article, titled "A Visit to the Slave Mother Who Killed Her Child," published in the *American Baptist* in 1856:

She [Margaret Garner] said that when the officers and slave-holders came to the house in which they were concealed, she caught a shovel and struck two of her children on the head, and she took a knife and cut the throat of the third, and tried to kill the other—that if they had given her time, she would have killed them all—that with regard to herself, she cared but little; but she was unwilling to have her children suffer as she had done.

I inquired if she was not excited almost to madness when she committed the act. No, she replied, I was as cool as I now am; and would much rather kill them at once, and thus end their sufferings, than have them taken back to slavery, and be murdered by piecemeal.

Morrison was moved to reconstruct imaginatively the life of Margaret Garner. Reflecting on that experience of slavery, she wrote: "I wondered if they [young blacks] knew the complicated psychic power one had to exercise to resist devastation."[4]

Morrison set herself the challenge of writing a revisionary slave narrative,

3. Andrew Levy, "Telling *Beloved,*" *Texas Studies in Literature and Language,* XXXIII (Spring, 1991), 117; Cathy Caruth, ed., *Trauma: Explorations in Memory* (Baltimore, Md., 1995), 4–5.

4. Toni Morrison, "Rediscovering Black History," *New York Times Magazine,* August 11, 1974, pp. 16, 18.

one that would do justice to Garner's stupendous act of resistance. Herself a scholar of this genre, Morrison summed up the limitations imposed on the nineteenth-century writer of the slave narrative: "it was extremely important" that "the writers of those narratives appear as objective as possible—not to offend the reader by being too angry, or by showing too much outrage." They had to be careful not to be inflammatory:

The milieu . . . dictated the purpose and the style. The narratives are instructive, moral and obviously representative. Some of them are patterned after the sentimental novel that was in vogue at the time. But whatever the level of eloquence or the form, popular taste discouraged the writers from dwelling too long or too carefully on the more sordid details of their experience. . . . Over and over, the writers pull the narrative up short with a phrase such as, "But let us drop a veil over these proceedings too terrible to relate." In shaping the experience to make it palatable to those who were in a position to alleviate it, they were silent about many things, and they "forgot" many things. There was a careful selection of the instances that they would record and a careful rendering of those that they chose to describe. . . . But, most importantly—at least for me—there was no mention of their interior life. For me, a writer in the last quarter of the twentieth century, not much more than a hundred years after Emancipation, a writer who is black and a woman—the exercise is very different. My job becomes how to rip that veil drawn over "proceedings too terrible to relate." The exercise is also critical for any person who is black, or who belongs to any marginalized category, for, historically, we were seldom invited to participate in the discourse even when we were its topic.[5]

Harriet Jacobs' autobiography, *Incidents in the Life of a Slave Girl*, gives examples of the blanks Morrison is attempting to fill in writing *Beloved*. Issues that Jacobs' narrative is only able to hint at or skim superficially Morrison's novel is able to explore in depth. Having read *Beloved*, one can hear and read the silences in Jacobs' story. We are more alert to her elisions, such as this one: "No pen can give an adequate description of the all-pervading corruption produced by slavery. . . . The lash and the foul talk of her master and his sons are her teachers."[6] In *Beloved*, Morrison is explicit about the white master, also called "school teacher," and his nephews' brutality and obscenity. Jacobs wrote

5. Toni Morrison, "The Site of Memory," in *Inventing the Truth: The Art and Craft of Memoir,* ed. William Zinsser (Boston, 1987), 109–11.

6. Harriet Jacobs, *Incidents in the Life of a Slave Girl* (New York, 1973), 51. Subsequent references will be cited as *Incidents* with page numbers within parentheses in the text.

that when Dr. Flint, her abusive master, learned that she was going to be a mother, "he was like a restless spirit from the pit": "He came every day; and I was subjected to such insults as no pen can describe. I would not describe them if I could; they were too low, too revolting" (*Incidents*, 79). In contrast, Morrison is explicit about the rape of the maternal body: school teacher and his nephews steal Sethe's milk, and after putting her pregnant stomach in a hole in the ground (to save the unborn slave), lash her back. Anne Goldman suggestively connects the theft of Sethe's milk to the appropriation of Sethe's ink by school teacher: "both the body and the word become commodified," "texts upon which the white man makes his mark."[7] It is this scene of the theft that drives her husband Halle insane because, as Jacobs wrote, "the husband of a slave has no power to protect her" (*Incidents*, 37). The fear of offending the sensibilities of her white audience and the fear of being judged by the prevailing (double) standards of womanly conduct prevented Jacobs from giving an adequate representation of her brutal experience; she could only say: "Slavery is terrible for men; but it is far more terrible for women. Superadded to the burden common to all, *they* have wrongs, and sufferings, and mortifications peculiarly their own" (*Incidents*, 79).

Morrison is able to demonstrate the truth of Jacobs' statement by focusing on every phase of a slave woman's life, from infancy to childhood, from girlhood to motherhood, and on to old age. *Beloved* makes brutally clear that aside from the "equality of oppression" that black men and women suffered, black women were also oppressed as *women*.[8] They were routinely subjected to rape, enforced childbirth, and natal alienation from their children. As Morrison's novel shows, physical abuse is humiliating, but the added emotional pain of a mother is devastating. Here, too, Jacobs held back, recounting without much emotion her brief reunion with her separated daughter in a short chapter entitled "The Meeting of Mother and Daughter." Margaret Garner's story enables Morrison to explore the passion of the slave mother and the anguish of the mother-child relationship. The grandmother character, Baby Suggs, amplifies Jacobs' grandmother, of whose nine children only one was left and of whom she wrote, "I

---

7. Anne E. Goldman, "I Made the Ink: (Literary) Production and Reproduction in *Dessa Rose* and *Beloved*," *Feminist Studies*, XVI (1990), 314.

8. For an illuminating analysis of the nature of the slave woman's oppression, see Angela Davis's essay "The Legacy of Slavery: Standards For A New Womanhood," in *Women, Race and Class* (New York, 1981), 3–29.

knew that she had been slowly murdered; and I felt that my troubles had helped to finish the work" (*Incidents*, 149). The pathos of Baby Suggs, whose resilient spirit is eventually broken, is captured by the image of her retiring to ponder on pieces of color. *Incidents*, like *Beloved*, is about a woman's persistent resistance to slavery: "My master had power and law on his side; I had a determined will. There is might in each" (*Incidents*, 87). Jacobs makes it clear, as does Margaret Garner, that for her it was either "freedom or the grave" (*Incidents*, 93).

Morrison also portrays the mother's deed as a heroic act of resistance, one among many that constituted the quotidian experience of slaves. Sethe's killing her child is not presented as an anomaly: Ella, the good woman of the town who assists Stamp Paid on the Underground Railroad, "had delivered, but would not nurse, a hairy white thing, fathered by 'the lowest yet,'" a white father and son who had held her in captivity and raped her; the child dies after five days of neglect. Sethe's mother abandoned the children white men forced upon her, keeping only Sethe, who is born of an African father; Sethe's mother "threw them all away but [her]. The one from the crew she threw away on the island. The others from more whites she also threw away."[9] By making resistance central to the experience of all slave women, not just the Nat Turners of history books, Morrison dissolves the stereotype of the mammy figure.

In *Beloved*, Morrison is interested in investigating the *cost* of such resistance, in exploring what the killing of the child did to the psyche of a mother like Margaret Garner. What is the psychological, emotional state of such an individual? Of the seven long years Harriet Jacobs spent in a garret hiding from her master—in a place so cramped she did not have room to stand, where she could hear her children but not reach out to them—we are told remarkably little. What must she have endured? It is *Beloved*, with its confinement of the reader to 124 Blue Stone Road and its inmates' interiority, that gives us some sense of what that experience might have been like in all its claustrophobic intensity. From the first lines of the novel ("124 was spiteful. Full of a baby's venom."), the reader is plunged *in medias res* into the haunted house and troubled memories of Morrison's characters. Now, a century later, it is possible for the black artist to remember, to grieve, to undertake the labyrinthine journey into unacknowledged regions of pain and anger and loss. As a race, it was expedient to

9. Toni Morrison, *Beloved* (New York, 1987), 259, 62. Subsequent references will be cited within parentheses in the text.

keep going, to forget. Observing that "nothing came down orally to my generation of that experience on the slave ship," Morrison attributed this collective
effacement of the past to "some survivalist intention to forget." It took Toni
Morrison's *Beloved* one hundred years to emerge; in the novel, it takes Sethe
eighteen years before she stops to linger over the crevices in the self, and when
she does, they engulf her. Remembering makes Sethe lose herself in the past
and lose her job. Historically, a beleaguered people could not afford to look
back; they had to keep going to meet the demands of the present. However,
self-preservation is not the only explanation for the delayed recall of the past,
which though forgotten remains latent. As Sethe's delayed response shows,
historical experience itself is a belated experience. Caruth's insight on this
matter is clarifying: "Since the traumatic event is not experienced as it occurs,
it is fully evident only in connection with another place, and in another time."[10]

Likewise, the representation of a historical trauma is belated, its articulation
relying on material and ideological conditions, such as the climate of literary
and political receptivity. In her discussion of the contemporary burgeoning of
historical novels by black women writers, Barbara Christian reminds us that
black women have written historical novels before, and that "there are pieces
written by African-American women during the periods about which . . .
contemporary novels are written."[11] The point to note is that they were un-
derwritten in some respects (reticent, masked, coded) and overwritten in others
(patterned after the sentimental novel).

Even when slavery (and its aftermath) is the subject of literature after
emancipation, the psychological pain of slavery is seldom dealt with; the focus
is on erasing the scene of colonial violation. Frances Harper, an active abolitionist and suffragist and daughter of free black parents, can only make brief
mention of the horror of slavery in her novel *Iola Leroy,* set in the Reconstruction period. A passing reference to the story of Margaret Garner is wedged into
an argument countering the heroine's schoolgirl notions about contented and
happy slaves. Far from feeling free to represent the brutality of slavery, Frances
Harper must make Iola an octoroon, almost white, and very naive so that she
may be more easily fused into the white reader's horizon. When Iola, a slaveholder's daughter, defends slavery, saying her father's slaves are content and do

10. Toni Morrison, in *Toni Morrison,* an RM Arts Production; (Chicago, 1987); Caruth,
Trauma, 8.

11. Christian, "'Somebody Forgot to Tell Somebody Something,'" 329.

not oppose the institution, her northern friend cites the case of Margaret Garner: "'I don't know,' was the response of her friend, 'but I do not think that that slave mother who took her four children, crossed the Ohio river on the ice, killed one of the children and attempted the lives of the other two, was a contented slave.'"[12] Harper does not explore the psychological dimensions of the characters who have emerged from slavery. Her novel is structured like a debate, with exemplary characters taking ideal stances. From Harper's point of view, the race is on trial; since the judges are biased, much energy is spent on presenting tidy resolutions, on proving that blacks could handle their freedom. Black families are sentimentally united and live a model life together in this novel subtitled *Shadows Uplifted*." Morrison, however, is in a position to resist the imperative to uplift and goes for the shadows. The family cohesion of *Iola Leroy* is shattered in *Beloved*, a novel that insists, "freeing yourself was one thing; claiming ownership of that freed self was another" (95).

In *Beloved*, set in 1873 and 1874, ten years after Emancipation, Morrison's characters slowly begin to take stock of the past. In most slave narratives, the past, its typicalness and inhumanity having been sketched, is something to leave behind. Charting the journey back from the free present to the slave past, *Beloved* reverses the progressive movement of the slave narrative. Further, while the slave narrative privileged the individual's account of coming to selfhood—in which the single, heroic self is fixed in the "I" of the subject and the tale ends with the victory of freedom—Morrison's narrative removes the individual from its center, giving way to a multiplicity of voices. *Beloved* invokes the "polyphonic ideal" of Mikhail Bakhtin, who in articulating the sociological poetics of the novel envisions "the ideal of the coexistence, interaction, and interdependence of several different, relatively autonomous consciousnesses that express simultaneously the various contents of the world within the unity of a single text." In *Beloved*, the memories are as complex as the people who tell, repeat, and improvise them; narrative becomes a collective, interactive enterprise. The effect of several individuals dealing with their pasts is a collective remembrance and purging. Ashraf H. A. Rushdy observed that in Morrison's novels, *Beloved* in particular, "memory exists as a communal property of

12. Harper, *Iola Leroy*, 98. Frances Harper, who spoke in Ohio against the Fugitive Bill, wrote a spirited poem about Margaret Garner, "The Slave Mother: A Tale of the Ohio." Establishing Garner's love for her children in the first half of the poem, Harper portrays the mother in the remaining half as a "heroic" and "mournful mother."

friends, of family, of a people. The magic of memory is that it is interpersonal, that it is the basis for constructing relationships with the other who also remembers."[13]

Organized by fragments coming together, the novel is about healing the self and uniting the traumatized individual with the community. Denver and Beloved both experience themselves as fragmenting bodies whose parts do not hold together; Paul D regards Sethe as the woman who can gather all the pieces of himself and arrange them in the right order for him. The narrative represents fragmented bodies, psyches, stories, and memories gradually becoming whole through telling. Like Sethe's wedding dress stitched from joining scraps of cloth, the novel is a collage of memories pieced together. Just as Baby Suggs heals Sethe's bruised body by bathing it part by part, Morrison heals the collective body of pain by the ritual of naming. The circular movement of the narrative both repeats and makes whole. The structure of time is in keeping with the idea of interiority: the unexpected eruption of traumatic memory, triggered by sensory stimuli, combines with the repetitiveness of oral narration. Salman Rushdie's comments on the "shape of the oral narrative" apply to *Beloved*: "It's not linear. An oral narrative does not go from the beginning to the middle to the end of the story. It goes in great swoops, it goes in spirals or in loops, it every so often reiterates something that happened earlier to remind you, and then takes you off again." As Sethe herself notes about her own narration: "She was spinning. . . . Circling, circling, now she was gnawing something else instead of getting to the point. . . . Sethe knew that the circle she was making around the . . . subject, would remain one" (161–63). Native American writer Paula Gunn Allen spoke in remarkably similar terms on cyclic time and narrative structure in her work: "There's a meandering, there are circles, but the circles aren't going in a nice perfect little spiral. Instead, they circle here, then they go over there and they circle, and they go someplace else and they circle, and the circles get bigger—until finally the whole thing is wrapped up, in some sense. It's an ever expanding, eccentric, erratic meandering spiral."[14]

13. Robert Anchor, "Bakhtin's Truths of Laughter," *Clio*, XIV, (1985), 253; Ashraf H. A. Rushdy, "'Rememory': Primal Scenes and Constructions in Toni Morrison's Novels," *Contemporary Literature*, XXXI (1990), 321–22.

14. Salmon Rushdie, in an interview in *The Empire Writes Back: Theory and Practice in Post-Colonial Literatures*, ed. Bill Ashcroft, Gareth Griffiths, and Helen Tiffin (London, 1989), 183–84; Paula Gunn Allen, "A MELUS Interview: Paula Gunn Allen," conducted by Franchot Ballinger and Brian Swann, *MELUS*, X (Summer, 1983), 21–22.

As in all Morrison's novels, the reader must participate in making the text cohere. Ruing the standards of conventional historiography, Michel de Certeau observed that "in its struggle against genealogical storytelling, the myths and legends of the collective memory, and the meanderings of the oral tradition, historiography establishes a certain distance between itself and common assertion and belief."[15] Morrison's *Beloved* reveals the depth that historiography loses as a result of that distance.

Beloved was conceived psychologically, fueled by the question of how to reclaim the freed self, body and soul. The plot is structured by the Freudian principle of "the return of the repressed": the tormented spirit of the past comes to possess the principal characters. Caruth, speaking of "the deeply disturbing insight into the enigmatic relation between trauma and survival" that Freud enabled, makes the point that "for those who undergo trauma, it is not only the moment of the event, but of the passing out of it that is traumatic; that survival itself, in other words, can be a crisis."[16] The survivors are possessed, and the only genuine exorcism is a collective hearing.

As the inscribed dedication to "Sixty Million / and more" indicates, the writing of the novel was an act of reparation. The novel reopens the psychic crypt of the past, and it is able to do so by an affirmation of its discredited world view. In this the novelist reflects to the historian the receptivity necessary for apprehending the past. In *Beloved*, Morrison introduces "awe and reverence and mystery and magic" because she is "deadly serious about fidelity to the milieu out of which [she] writes[s] and in which [her] ancestors actually lived." The plot of the novel deals with the possession of 124 Blue Stone Road and its inmates—Sethe and her daughter Denver—by a ghost whose eventual exorcism brings peace. In the nineteenth-century African American ethos Morrison re-creates, the presence of the ghost is taken seriously. The reader is required, from the first line of the novel, to suspend disbelief and to enter the house understanding that it is haunted. The cupboard shakes, a doleful red aura surrounds the door, and small anomalous incidents accumulate over time to establish the identity of the spirit: the "crawling already" baby girl who is buried beneath the pink stone inscribed with the word "Beloved." The possession is not a singular occurrence, for Baby Suggs says that houses of negroes all over

15. Certeau, *Heterologies*, 200.
16. Caruth, *Trauma*, 9.

the land were peopled by ghosts: "Not a house in the country ain't packed to its rafters with some dead Negro's grief" (5). According to West African belief, the dead are not finished with the living because the past (the dead), present (the living), and future (the unborn) are coexistent. Deceased ancestors can and do communicate with their descendants, especially if certain rites for the dead have not been performed. Such a world view posits a fluidity and continuity between the past and present, and fidelity to this milieu gives Morrison the latitude to move freely between the literal and the metaphorical. The character Beloved is what the Yoruba would call "Abiku," a "wanderer child," "the same child who dies and returns again and again to plague the mother."[17]

Beloved grafts a West African religious world view to a Christian one whose biblical cadences and echoes are present in an altered meaning. As Lerone Bennett, Jr., points out, "the slaves reinterpreted white patterns, weaving a whole new universe around biblical images and giving a new dimension and new meaning to Christianity." Their God was not the one who demanded of servants obedience to their masters, but the one who "delivered the Israelites"; the influence of Christianity "was only one element in a complex world view that included spirits that were not visible to white Christians. . . . Many American slaves believed in Jesus *and* an overlapping world of spirits who could be manipulated and persuaded to serve the living. . . . In a total and passionate quest for *this* God, the slaves . . . turned American Christianity inside out, like a glove, infusing it with African-oriented melodies and rhythms and adding new patterns, such as the ring shout, ecstatic seizure and communal, call-and-response patterns. . . . The emblem of this creation was the invisible black church of slavery, which centered in the portable 'hush-harbors.'"[18] Grandmother "Baby Suggs, holy" has her own hush-harbor in "the Clearing," where communal praying, singing, crying, and dancing merge together in a collective, ceremonial act of healing. In the novel, various verses from the Bible are given new meaning: the transmutation from the word "Beloved" inscribed on the tombstone to the living Beloved reinterprets the Gospel According to St. John: "And the Word was made flesh, and dwelt among us" (1:14). "I am my beloved's, and my beloved is mine" (Song of Songs 6:3) becomes "I am Beloved and she

17. Morrison, "The Site of Memory," 111; Wole Soyinka, "Abiku," *Idanre and Other Poems* (New York, 1987), 28–30.

18. Lerone Bennett, Jr., *Before the Mayflower: A History of Black America* (New York, 1984), 99, 102.

is mine" (210). Sethe trying to appease the hungry Beloved enacts the truth of the biblical statement "Many waters cannot quench love,"—or the lack of love—"neither can the floods drown it: if a man would give all the substance of his house for love, it would utterly be contemned" (Song of Songs 8:7). Sethe does give all her substance to Beloved, who feeds on her and is still unsatisfied. The novel is an evocation of "The Witness of the Spirit" in The First Letter of John: "This is he that came by water and blood, *even* Jesus Christ, not by water only but by water and blood. And it is the Spirit that beareth witness, because the Spirit is truth" (5:6). The novel subverts the male trinity with the female one of mother, daughter, and sad ghost. Speaking of Beloved, Ella tells Stamp Paid, "You know as well as I do that people who die bad don't stay in the ground." Stamp "couldn't deny it. Jesus Christ Himself didn't" (188). Beloved, who dies bad so that she, her mother, and her sister may be redeemed from bondage, is the resurrected.

According to West African belief, the dead live as long as they are remembered. In the novel, storytelling, remembering, and retelling the past become ways of feeding the hungry and neglected dead. Beloved, the ghost demanding attention, is both thirsty and hungry. Hers is a sensual hunger for Sethe: looking, hearing, and touching are food to her starved senses. Above all, storytelling is the food Beloved craves from both Denver and Sethe. The appeasement of physical hunger is interchanged with the aural intake of story and song. By the end of the novel, the well-fed ghost leaves with a "big belly," evidence of Sethe's nourishing her. Here, as in the rest of the novel, the meaning is literal and metaphorical.

Indeed, the complexity of the novel stems from the fact that it constantly merges the physical and the psychical, the literal and the metaphorical. The arrivals and departures of Beloved easily lend themselves to a metaphorical reading. The novel begins in 1873 at Sethe's house, haunted ever since she killed her baby daughter rather than let her be taken back to slavery in accordance with the Fugitive Slave Act. Both Sethe and her other daughter Denver are used to the presence of the ghost, whom they accept as being not evil but sad. They live their lives in resigned solitude under a pervasive gloom. It is only when Paul D meets Sethe after eighteen years of separation that the past and present are stirred to life. Each recalls for the other buried images and tumultuous emotions connected to their slave days. Each also brings the other hope for the future. After Paul D touches her back, which is etched with scars resembling a branching tree and numb to any sensation, Sethe wonders if she should "feel the hurt her back ought to"; she feels she can "trust things and remember things because the last of the Sweet Home men was there to catch her if she sank." But as she thought these thoughts, "the house itself was pitching" and Paul D was physically fighting an invisible adversary; he "did not stop . . . until everything was rock quiet," until "it was gone" (18). A connection is made between the opening of Sethe's scarred back and the rocking of the house, a site of interiority: "Merely kissing the wrought iron on her back had shook the house, had made it necessary for him to beat it to pieces" (20). Paul D is activating, or letting loose, the past; the ghost leaves the house in *spirit* but returns in the *figure* of Beloved, assuming real-life proportions, becoming a concrete shape to contend with. Sethe realizes there had been "no room for any other thing or body until Paul D arrived and broke up the place, making room, shifting it" (39). It is Paul D who ushers in Beloved by asking Sethe, who is unsure about making room for him in her life, "What about inside?" "I don't go inside," replies Sethe. Paul D reassures her: "Go as far inside as you need to, I'll hold your ankles. Make sure you get back out" (46). Going inside is like embarking on a voyage through the underworld, remembering beyond the river of forgetfulness back to life.

However, it is not a one-way influence; if Paul D makes the tree of death on Sethe's back stir with life, Sethe in turn moves Paul D. As he knows, "this was not a normal woman in a normal house. As soon as he had stepped through the red light he knew that, compared to 124, the rest of the world was bald." After his soul-numbing experience in the underground slave camp of Alfred, Georgia, "he had shut down a generous portion of his head, operating on the part that helped him walk, eat, sleep, sing." With the pleasure of seeing Sethe, however, "the closed portion of his head opened like a greased lock" (41). Since Sethe, too, makes him grapple with his past, the flesh-and-blood Beloved is the spirit of the past that touches them both. For Paul D is literally and figuratively moved by Beloved. Sweet Home, Kentucky, and Alfred, Georgia, are settings of past experiences traumatic enough to keep him moving, make him a restless, wandering man unable to be still in one place. In 124, Beloved starts him moving again, this time involuntarily—he genuinely wishes to settle down with Sethe, to make a life with her. Paul D experiences Beloved as a mysterious force exerted upon him. The past will not let him rest; the unresolved, unacknowledged pain from slavery will not allow him to form a stable relationship with Sethe.

Paul D is peeved by the timing of Beloved's appearance: "She had appeared and been taken in on the very day Sethe and he had patched up their quarrel, gone out in public and had a right good time—like a family" (66). However, before Sethe and Paul D can create an emotional space for each other, they must deal with the past. The haste with which Paul D and Sethe move toward love-making—"It was over before they could get their clothes off"(20)—is necessarily followed by a slow period of self-recovery. This is particularly critical for Sethe, who has undergone a terrible trauma. So, Beloved is the unresolved past that comes between them; for both Sethe and Paul D, she is the return of the repressed. The haunted state of their minds is made clear when they first make love; both are caught up in their own memories. Though these do converge sensuously in the image of the corn flowing with juice and though they have much to share, judging by their mutual disappointment, they are not yet ready for each other. If Sethe is numb to physical touch—the white master's infliction of brutal pain has made her block her capacity to feel—Paul D's own heart is described as a tobacco tin of memories shut tight with a rusty lid. He has to *recover* his heart: "by the time he got to 124 nothing in this world could pry it open" (113). Sethe succeeds in loosening the lid, as does Beloved; her voice is the past confronting Paul D in the coldhouse: "You have to touch me. On the inside part. And you have to call me my name" (117). Metaphorically, in touching Beloved, Paul D is touching the past inside him and is in the process of being healed: the lid of his rusty tobacco tin has been dislodged, and as the tightly guarded content of the past is spilling out, he begins to find his "red heart."

Beloved is reminiscent of Jung's archetype of the maiden, who is "often described as not altogether human in the usual sense; she is either of unknown or peculiar origin, or she looks strange or undergoes strange experiences, from which one is forced to infer the maiden's extraordinary, myth-like character." Archetypes are "living psychic forces that demand to be taken seriously"; having an "unconscious core of meaning," "an archetypal content expresses itself, first and foremost, in metaphors." First seen as mermaid with hair like fish, Beloved is associated with that liminal zone between land and water: the bridge. If, metaphorically speaking, Beloved is desire—a black Aphrodite rising from the waters of the unconscious, a "fully dressed woman [who] walked out of the water" (50)—she is also a plausible character with a specific past who enables Morrison to introduce the Middle Passage. Richard Jackson situates *Beloved* along with Gayl Jones's *Song for Anninho* in the context of "Middle Passage literature" by Latin American black writers such as Afro-Cuban Nancy Morejon, Afro-Columbian Manuel Zapata Olivella, and Carlos Guilermo Wilson, all of whom "combat the stigma associated with the black slave past."[19]

In the nonfigurative reading, Beloved is a child who is captured with her mother in Africa and packed with other slaves on a ship making the voyage over the Atlantic. When her mother apparently jumps ship (it was not uncommon for slaves to commit suicide) the child is left deeply disturbed by her disappearance. We can imagine what happens to her afterward from her monologue and from Sethe's surmise, which corroborates Stamp Paid's hearsay about a white man imprisoning a girl. Sethe "believed Beloved had been locked up by some whiteman for his own purposes, and never let out the door. Then she must have escaped to a bridge or someplace and rinsed the rest out of her mind" (119). Stamp Paid recalls a tale about "a girl locked up in the house with a whiteman over by Deer Creek. Found him dead last summer and the girl gone. Maybe that's her. Folks say he had her in there since she was a pup" (235). We are led to assume that she escapes and comes to a bridge, from which she peers into the water and sees images of her mother's disappearing face. Her development has been arrested at an early stage; her self-image is deeply fragmented: she has no face of her own because the mother in whose eyes the child would become whole has left her. She jumps in after the image of her mother and emerges from the stream near 124 Blue Stone, where she fixes upon Sethe's face. She is taken in by Sethe as a stranger in need of food and rest. Sethe's daughter Denver, in her profound loneliness, clings to Beloved as the drowning will a boat. That Beloved, Denver, and Sethe should emotionally spiral into each other is inevitable. Each serves to fulfill the deepest, most dire need of the other. For Denver—who is desolate since her two brothers ran away in terror, whose ears voluntarily shut out sound for two years to compensate for hearing the terrible story of her sister's death at the hands of her own mother, and who is even more lonely since grandma Baby Suggs's death—Beloved is a savior.

Like Paul D and Sethe, Beloved is a character who is haunted by a traumatic past and compelled to relive different moments of it. On being asked by Denver about her name, she replies, "In the dark my name is Beloved" (75). Her driving

19. Jung, *The Archetypes and the Collective Unconscious*, 186, 156, 157; Richard Jackson, "Remembering the 'Dismembered': Modern Black Writers and Slavery in Latin America," *Callaloo*, XIII (1990), 142. Jackson also noted that Morrison went to Brazil to research slave records for her novel.

Paul D out of Sethe's house to the coldhouse and cornering him there to touch her and call her by her name may be variously interpreted. Morrison may be revising the Oedipus story—it is not the father but the mother the daughter seeks—though Beloved does seek out Paul D. She tells him that it is Sethe's face that she wants: "I don't love nobody but her" (116). Her trips to the coldhouse seem to be governed by the desire to drive a wedge between Paul D and Sethe; by seducing him, she intends to shame him and weaken his claim on Sethe. When she is with Denver in the damp coldhouse, Beloved relives the trauma of the slave ship: "I'm like this," she demonstrates, and "bends over, curls up and rocks." All she says is, "Over there. Her face" (124). Beloved is a disturbed personality, a nubile girl whose mind is unable to absorb the layers of shock her body has been subjected to since childhood.

It is not until later, after Paul D confronts Sethe with the old newspaper clipping and leaves, that Beloved's identity as a ghost is confirmed by a Sethe driven in upon herself; under the emotional strain she begins to see Beloved as her own baby girl returned to her. "When the click came Sethe didn't know what it was" (175). But the click, "the settling of pieces into places," comes after Paul D confronts Sethe with the notorious paper clipping from eighteen years ago and accuses her of behaving like an animal, of having four feet, not two. It is then that she welcomes Beloved as her own daughter. The narrator remarks, "things were where they ought to be or poised and ready to glide in" (176). Now, after the desolation of Paul D's departure, Sethe has something to look forward to: she is "eager to lie down and unravel the proof for the conclusion she had already leapt to" (181). The desire to believe precedes the proof. Events of the past are recast in the light of this desire, so that "the hand-holding shadows she had seen on the road were not Paul D, Denver and herself, but 'us three'" (182). After convincing her that "there was a world out there," Paul D leaves her to shrink her world to the confines of her room. Echoing the novel's epigraph, Sethe calls her Beloved who is not her Beloved. Sethe wants to believe Beloved is her daughter come back to her from the dead because it gives her a chance to explain her actions and demonstrate her love. It means that forgiveness, her redemption, is at hand.

Marianne Hirsch rightly points out that "the psychoanalytic plot has . . . silenced the mother's response to separation" and that what is left is "an untold maternal experience": "Even as feminist theorizing, based in psychoanalysis, urges feminists to shift their political allegiance back from father to mother, even as it urges us to sympathize with our mothers' position in patriarchy, it is still . . . written from the child's primary process perspective: permeated with desires for the mother's approval, with fear of her power, and with anger and resentment at her powerlessness." Morrison invokes and revises the mother-daughter story of Demeter and Persephone. Pluto, god of the underworld in Greek mythology, is envisioned as *dark*; his abduction of Persephone to the underworld causes the earth mother Demeter to mourn the loss of her daughter. In *Beloved*, *white* men take captive the daughter of the African mother gathering flowers; the same sundering is true for Sethe and her mother. C. G. Jung theorized: "The psyche pre-existent to consciousness (e.g., in the child) participates in the maternal psyche on the one hand, while on the other it reaches across to the daughter psyche. We could therefore say that every mother contains her daughter in herself and every daughter her mother, and that every woman extends backwards into her mother and forward into her daughter."[20] The mother's language and the love that flows with her milk are both denied Sethe, who in turn grows up to be a mother whose *daughter*'s milk is stolen from her.

This lack binding mother and daughter is as painful as Paul D's nonverbal communication with other slave men through the chain, "the best hand-forged chain in Georgia" (107). However, Paul D is left out of the vortex of mother-daughter guilt and pain; he cannot decipher their code. As Jung remarks, the Demeter-Persephone myth "exists on the plane of mother-daughter experience, which is alien to man and shuts him off"; in its formation "the feminine influence so far outweighed the masculine that the latter had practically no significance. The man's role in the Demeter myth is really only that of seducer or conqueror."[21] In a way, 124 must be evacuated by the men—no Howard, no Buglar, and no Paul D must be around—so that the suffering women endure by virtue of being women can take center stage, so that "when Sethe locked the door, the women inside were free at last to be what they liked, see whatever they saw and say whatever was on their minds" (199). One must note, however, that *Beloved* also portrays the black man's pain with great sensitivity. The painful memories of Paul D—the collar, the bit, the lynching, the enforced sodomy—create a composite picture of the male slave showing the breaking of

---

20. Marianne Hirsch, "Clytemnestra's Children," in *Alice Walker*, ed. Harold Bloom (New York, 1989), 200; Jung, *The Archetypes and the Collective Unconscious*, 188.

21. Jung, *The Archetypes and the Collective Unconscious*, 203, 184.

his spirit; a lame rooster, a cock called Mr., has more going for him than a black man. The account of Halle, the strong and responsible son and husband, finally breaking down at the sight of his wife being raped is moving; as Paul D insists, "A man ain't a goddamn ax. Chopping, hacking, busting every goddamn minute of the day. Things get to him. Things he can't chop down because they're inside" (69). Still, the emphasis in *Beloved* is upon the maternal trauma incurred under slavery.

When Julia Kristeva wrote that "a mother is a continuous separation, a division of the very flesh. And consequently a division of language,"[22] she did not have the slave mother in mind. She was referring to the mother who fell under the category *Woman*. Slavery puts into high relief every psychoanalytic feminist utterance describing women and the family in patriarchy. Paul D's cruel reminder to Sethe that she has two feet (human), not four (animal) refers to the brute fact that under slavery black women were listed under the category *Animal*, valued as breeders, not mothers. The extreme and unspeakable nature of the slave woman's oppression enables it, when spoken, to convulse the symbolic order of patriarchy. In doing so, *Beloved* lets us recognize the need for a historically specific differentiation of women's bodies, psyches, and oppressions. Kristeva's suggestive positing of a maternal semiotic, a pre-oedipal language preceding a child subject's formal acquisition of language, is complicated by this novel. Sethe remembers as a child hearing and speaking an African language, traces of which now elude her memory. Morrison does not (as Kristeva does) refer to a universally repressed, preverbal maternal semiotic but to a specific violence done to a mother language. In *Beloved*, not only is the mother tongue obliterated from consciousness, the actual tongue of the speaking subject is harnessed or clamped by an iron bit. Morrison's intense practice of language is an attempt to articulate the pain of this double violence.

Situated on Blue Stone Road, Sethe's house, and by extension *Beloved* (the house of fiction), has a blues tone—governed by what Wilson Harris calls "a blues muse, an ancient mother of scarred freedom/unfreedom." The language attempts to articulate the matrix of the slave woman's pain as mother, as daughter. When Stamp Paid passes by 124, he hears voices: "The speech wasn't nonsensical, exactly, nor was it tongues. But . . . he couldn't describe or cipher it to save his life" (172):

22. Julia Kristeva, "Stabat Mater," in *The Kristeva Reader*, ed. Toril Moi (New York, 1986), 178.

You are my face; I am you. Why did you leave me who am you?
I will never leave you again
Don't ever leave me again
You will never leave me again
You went in the water
I drank your blood
I brought your milk
You forgot to smile
I loved you
You hurt me
You came back to me
You left me (216–217)

As Houston Baker, Jr., notes, "A matrix is a womb, a network, a rock bearing embedded fossils, a *rocky trace of a gemstone's removal*." It is the absence, separation, or forceful removal of a daughter from her mother, of a mother from her daughter, that constitutes the core of *Beloved*.[23] Baby Suggs and her daughter-in-law Sethe are both rocks bearing embedded fossils, the remains of the past. Beloved is the removed gemstone. That she is not an exception is suggested by the references to Baby Suggs's countless lost children.

Remembering and mourning become signs of the subject's agency and recovery. Sections of *Beloved* are like an elegy: "the process of mourning has a kind of intrinsic rhythm." Freud defines sadness as "the most archaic expression of a non-symbolizable unnameable narcissistic wound." In her piece on mourning, Alice Koller answers the question "What is it to mourn?": "It is to be hurled into pain so vast that . . . it usurps all other thinking, all other feeling, a pain that occupies you as you occupy the house you live in." The residence at 124 Blue Stone Road is indeed occupied territory; Beloved, who occupies the house, is the very embodiment of pain, which is also an unexpressed rage. Koller tracks the language of *mourning* etymologically through various languages, noting that "these derivations from language to language carry living seed": "'Mourn' from Greek for 'care,' in turn relating to 'memory,' 'remembering.' 'Pain' from Greek for 'payment,' 'penalty'; 'to pay,' 'to punish'; 'price.' 'Grief' from Latin and from Greek for 'heavy.' 'Grieve,' from Middle English, Old French, Latin for 'to

23. Wilson Harris, *Womb of Space: The Cross-Cultural Imagination* (Westport, Conn., 1983), 28; Houston Baker, *Blues, Ideology, and Afro-American Literature: A Vernacular Theory* (Chicago, 1985), 13, italics mine.

burden,' from Latin for 'heavy,' 'grave,' like Gothic, Greek, Sanskrit for 'heavy.' 'Sorrow' from Middle English *sorow,* from Old English *sorg.* Like Old High German *sorga* 'sorrow,' and Old Slavic *sraga* 'sickness.' 'Anguish' from Latin for 'straits,' for 'narrow,' like Old English for 'narrow.'" As Morrison remarked in an interview, in her treatment of slavery she wanted to do something narrow and deep instead of attempting the breadth of historical accounts. This narrowing translates into a sustained and mournful commemoration of the past; Sethe's sorrow is "a permeating heaviness that constricts [her] doings to one single doing: trying to match the present absence with the past presence, and failing, remembering."[24]

The individual ego is defenseless against the unbuffered assault of the repressed. After the initial joy of discovering each other wears off, Beloved's recriminations begin and Sethe cannot apologize enough. There is no filling the void of the irreparable damage done to Beloved or the deep guilt that plagues Sethe. Sethe relinquishes control, her job, her sanity, "broken down, finally, from trying to take care of and make up for" (243). Denver has been locked out of the mother-daughter gaze of Sethe and Beloved, who are "locked in a love" that is draining them, driving them to "the edge of violence, then over." Their roles change: Sethe "was like a chastized child while Beloved ate up her life," the past in danger of engulfing the present (250).

The plot, built on the principle of the return of the repressed, reenacts, with a saving difference, the fatal configuration of events that took place eighteen years before. With the desperate realization that her mother's life is in danger, Denver is galvanized into taking charge and leaving her mother's house to seek help. When news of the ghost's revenge on Sethe reaches the community, they intervene. Led by Ella, thirty women gather outside the house to pray. Although times have changed and the situation that brings a white man driving a carriage to 124 is benevolent—Mr. Bodwin, the abolitionist who had appealed on behalf of Sethe, is coming to take Denver to her first day of work at his house—Sethe is locked in the past and memory of danger makes her fly on reflex to attack the approaching man. Fortunately, the community

24. J. Hillis Miller, "Symposium," *Rhetoric and Form: Deconstruction at Yale,* ed. Robert Con Davis and Ronald Schleifer (Norman, 1985), 97; Sigmund Freud, "Mourning and Melancholia," in *On Metapsychology* (Harmondsworth, Eng., 1964), 251–68, Vol. XI of *The Pelican Freud Library;* Alice Koller, *The Stations of Solitude* (New York, 1990), 307, 308; *Toni Morrison,* an RM Arts Production.

of women and Denver save her from herself. Beloved, who has been standing naked on the porch holding Sethe's hand, is also prey to the past; in Sethe's sudden departure from her, in the crowd of black people, she is reminded of the hold of the slave ship; in the white face of Mr. Bodwin she sees "the man without skin, looking . . . at her" (262). She flees the scene that unfolds the horror of her past.

The reader doesn't know what becomes of Beloved, whether she lives or dies, but can assume hers is a tragic end. She is pregnant and deranged, naked and defenseless; little good is likely to befall her. Her missing figure links this novel to the next one, *Jazz.* (Indeed, it is tempting to think of Beloved's continuity in the figure of Wild, the mad woman in the cane that Joe Trace believes is his mother.) However, at the metaphorical level, Beloved is gone because the past she represents has been confronted; by facing the past, Sethe is released into the present. Beloved disappears, having served her function of "rememory"; the sound and fury is over, and spiteful, loud 124 is finally quiet. Paul D may lay his story beside Sethe's. Beloved goes as she comes; the unaccountability of her whereabouts, her physical absence, constitutes the experience of loss at the heart of slavery. Like the footprints that fit everyone's feet, Beloved is the past of those ordinary unheralded lives silenced in history. Like Denver, the author "construct[s] out of the strings she had heard all her life a net to hold Beloved" (76). But the past is infinite, and Beloved slips out again.

In a way it is important that Beloved remain somewhat inaccessible and mysterious so as to be a suggestive symbol of the unconscious, of desire, of the past, of memory—for none of these is fully graspable by the conscious mind. The "thunderblack" pregnant figure of Beloved, alive in the figure of Wild in *Jazz,* is also an evocative figure of Mnemosyne and of the muse of the black woman artist: it is in search of the mother's garden (Alice Walker's phrase) that the black woman writes her story. In *Jazz,* the narrator confesses being touched and released by this matrix figure: She (the "woman who lived in a rock") "has seen me and is not afraid of me. She hugs me. Understands me. Has given me her hand. I am touched by her. Released in secret."[25]

If the task of the novel has been to lift the "veil behind the veil" that has been "disremembered and unaccounted for" and "deliberately forgot," it must also eventually draw the veil (274). Morrison covers the exposed wound of the past with the repeated statement, "It was not a story to pass on" (275). The

25. Toni Morrison, *Jazz* (New York, 1992), 221.

writer is careful to note at the end that in history or narrative, all cannot be accounted for; there remains that which remains unspoken, locked. The gaps and silences become quietly recriminating, refuting the possibility of any post-humous recompense that claims to be adequate to the past. We are left with an image of a lock, "a latch latched" and covered with the "apple-green bloom" of lichen. At a certain point, authorial control gives way to unaccountability and, metaphorically, to the agency of natural elements: the night, the rain, the wind: "The rest is weather" (275). The image of the weathered lock signals a closure, reminding us that for survival, forgetting is as important as remember-ing. But this forgetting is not an act of the unconscious. It is the forgetting enabled by a therapeutic working-through of the repressed material of historical trauma.

6

A HEARING OF HISTORY:

Jazz

The belated experience of trauma . . . suggests that history is
not only the passing on of a crisis but also the passing on of a
survival that can only be possessed within a history larger than
any single individual or any single generation.

—Cathy Caruth, *Unclaimed Experience*

The traumatized . . . carry an impossible history within them, or they become
themselves the symptom of a history that they cannot entirely possess." It is
this impossible history carried by Morrison's characters that makes them erupt
from the text with such force. And precisely because it is a certain historical
realization that Morrison is after, no single character dominates her novels.
The theme of trauma unfolding with such persistence through *Beloved* finds its
sequel in *Jazz*, a novel that also hearkens back to *The Bluest Eye*. Both these
novels begin by casually presenting the listener with the facts of a hard case.
In *The Bluest Eye*, Pecola is having her father's baby. In *Jazz*, the narrative
voice gossips about Joe shooting his eighteen-year-old lover, Dorcas, and about
his wife, Violet, running to deface the corpse. In both novels, alarming facts
call for interpretation. The reader is quickly informed by the narrator of *Jazz*
that no juridical or charitable agencies could understand or help the situation:
"the dead girl's aunt [Alice Manfred] didn't want to throw money to helpless
lawyers or laughing cops," and the Salem Women's Club, with more destitute
cases at hand, "left Violet to figure out on her own what the matter was and
how to fix it." Violet's is also the position of the reader. We are left to figure
out the case as it is presented through an ensemble of voices: solos, duets, and
trios mediated by the narrator's voice. The narrator's displacement of the scene

of death implies that it is not what constitutes the *meaning* of trauma. What is traumatic is what is being repeated in that scene: the violent past left behind by Joe and Violet that has been remembered or repeated pathologically. Thus the enigma of the novel's present becomes a place of departure, for the search for an answer that can only be found in a retrospective and collective telling. In the resilience of Joe and Violet, in their individual survival, lies the historic meaning of a collective destruction. "It is through the peculiar and paradoxical complexity of survival that the theory of individual trauma contains within it the core of the trauma of a larger history."[1]

In its work of understanding and integrating the dissonance of the past, *Jazz* continues the project of *Beloved*. While *Beloved* explicates the experience of slavery and its aftermath, *Jazz* spans the period from 1855 to 1926. Both narratives submit to a repetition compulsion in order to heal the collective body stricken by memory that has not been worked through. In both novels, the deadly determinings of the past are deterred in the present by an act of understanding. *Jazz*, like the music it is named for, is a complex emotional and cognitive performance aimed at the collective heart of its audience. It is narrated from the site of trauma—the place of the stuck record. But in order to release the present from the grip of the past, the characters and the reader are compelled to collectively audition the dissonance, to acknowledge the traumatic nature of the past. It reconstitutes the social history of America by constructing historical knowledge from the vantage point of its oppressed players. As Satya Mohanty points out, "Granting the possibility of epistemological privilege to the oppressed might be more than a sentimental gesture; in many cases in fact it is the only way to push us toward greater social objectivity."[2]

Just as *Beloved* was inspired by the true story of Margaret Garner, *Jazz* is based on a real event. In his review of *Jazz*, Henry Louis Gates, Jr., gives this account:

Morrison first came across the story of the star-crossed lovers when she read Camille Billops' manuscript, *The Harlem Book of the Dead*, which contains photographs and commentary by the great African-American photographer James Van Der Zee and

---

1. Caruth, *Trauma*, 4; Morrison, *Jazz*, 4 (subsequent references will be cited within parentheses in the text); Cathy Caruth, *Unclaimed Experience: Trauma, Narrative, and History* (Baltimore, 1996), 71.

2. Mohanty, "The Epistemic Status of Cultural Identity," 72.

poems by Owen Dodson. Van Der Zee described . . . the curious origins of his photograph of a young woman's corpse in this manner: "She was the one I think was shot by her sweetheart at a party with a noiseless gun. She complained of being sick at the party and friends . . . [took] her in the room and laid her down. After they undressed her and loosened her clothes, they saw the blood on her dress. They asked her about it and she said, "I'll tell you tomorrow, yes, I'll tell you tomorrow." She was just trying to give him a chance to get away.

Gates also quotes a poem by Owen Dodson inspired by the incident: "They lean over me and say: / "Who deathed you who / who, who, who, who . . . / I whisper: "Tell you presently." Toni Morrison's narrative makes no secret of who deathed whom—the question is not who. As in the conversation between Alice and Violet, the questions are:

> "Why did [Joe Trace] do such a thing?"
> "Why did [Dorcas]?"
> "Why did [Violet]?" (81)

Though the question of who deathed whom is easily answered, it remains a large and complex question pertaining to American history that *Jazz* attempts posthumously and circuitously to answer. Just as Alice knows that Dorcas' case cannot be settled by the judiciary, so Morrison implies that the question of history cannot be settled in history books or in law courts. Such a question demands a different kind of hearing by a collective ear—an ethical listening that the narrative of *Jazz* both demands and prepares us for. Further, Morrison prevents a reading of the case in terms of individual pathology. As Peter Lyman points out, human suffering cannot be treated as though it were an issue of personality: "A psychology of suffering would have to understand guilt, anxiety, depression or hysteria as suppressed social relations. . . . Psychology serves the interests of the hegemony when it strips human experience of its collective and active character, and conceals oppression by blaming the victims for their symptoms."[3] The novel becomes an extended melodic reverie on the makings of desire, on the indirect paths of its thwarted rhythms in historic time.

Jazz is about the function of narrative as secular revelation. Such belief in

---

3. Henry Louis Gates, Jr., in *Toni Morrison: Critical Perspectives Past and Present*, ed. K. A. Appiah (New York, 1993), 52–53; Peter Lyman, qtd. in Marianne Hirsch, "Clytemnestra's Children," in *Alice Walker*, ed. Bloom, 210.

revelation is in keeping with the epigraph, "I am the name of the sound / and the sound of the name," taken from the poetic tract "The Thunder, Perfect Mind" found in the ancient Nag Hammadi texts (twelve books in Coptic script discovered this century in Upper Egypt). "The Thunder, Perfect Mind" is believed to be a revelation given by a female power or goddess whose being is an unfathomable mystery. In the words of George MacRae, it is "a revelation discourse delivered by a female revealer in the first person," also containing "various exhortations to hear and reflect, and reproaches for failing to do so." We can appreciate how Morrison absorbs this figure into the persona of her narrator, who is designated by the sound and name of jazz. Further, the unknown gnostic revelator's stance as a persecuted outsider (an Egyptian's relationship to the dominant Greco-Christian discourse?) allies her with the position of a female African American narrator of the 1920s. Consider these lines from "The Thunder, Perfect Mind" :

Why have you hated me in your counsels?
For I shall be silent among those who are silent,
    and I shall appear and speak.
Why then have you hated me, you Greeks?
    Because I am a barbarian among [the] barbarians?
For I am the wisdom [of the] Greeks
    and the knowledge of the barbarians.

The ancient one "who has been hated everywhere" and who declares, "I am peace, / and war has come because of me / And I am an alien and a citizen" becomes a perfect correlative for the narrator of post–Civil War, post-Reconstruction mayhem.[4]

"History is over, you all, and everything's ahead at last." The narrator, reflecting on the mood of "the City in 1926 when all the wars are over and there will never be another one," makes an ironic comment on the philosophy of the New Negro as envisioned by the leaders of the Harlem Renaissance: "At last, at last, everything's ahead. The smart ones say so and people listening to them and reading what they write down agree: Here comes the new. Look out. There goes the sad stuff. The bad stuff. The things-nobody-could-help-stuff. The way

4. George MacRae, Introduction to "The Thunder, Perfect Mind," in *The Nag Hammadi Library in English* (New York, 1977), 271, 273–75.

everybody was then and there. Forget that" (7). Here the smart ones are the educated elite and cosmopolitan literati of the Harlem Renaissance—among them Alain Locke, whose book *The New Negro* was published in 1925. As Samuel Floyd, Jr., noted, the "Talented Tenth" aspired to "transform black folk genres into high art"; however, the rural influx into the cities and the attendant music "was also the source of certain ambivalent attitudes on the part of the black leadership." To a self-conscious intelligentsia anxious to represent the race *and* to distance themselves both from the vulgarity of the masses and the white stereotype of black primitivism, the secular music of the black masses was incorrigible. As Hazel Carby observed, prior to World War I "the overwhelming majority of blacks were in the South, at a vast physical and metaphorical distance from those intellectuals who represent the interests of the race. After the war, black intellectuals had to confront the black masses on the streets of their cities and responded in a variety of ways." Different meanings competed for the sign of the New Negro. Zora Neale Hurston, for example, distinguished herself from the Harlem literati by embracing black folk culture. But, as Carby suggested, "a reconstruction of 'the folk'" elides the issue of "class confrontation of the Northern cities." There were radical organizations and "radical intellectuals like Asa Philip Randolph and Chandler Owen, editors of the *Messenger*," for whom the term *New Negro* signified "radical working class meaning."[5]

Where does Toni Morrison take her stand? She articulates, among other things, the split consciousness of the middle class as it confronted the times, through the image of Alice Manfred "balancing herself with two different hand gestures," one toward the music, one against (59). From genteel Alice's perspective, Joe and Violet were the "embarrassing kind" of Negro couple "she trained Dorcas away from" (79). Alice also "knew from sermons and editorials that [jazz] wasn't real music—just colored folks' stuff: harmful certainly; embarrassing, of course; but not real, not serious." Yet despite herself, Alice Manfred "swore she heard" in the reckless rhythms of urban displacement "a complicated anger . . . something hostile that distinguished itself as flourish and roaring seduction." The narrator as historian tells us: "It was impossible to keep the Fifth Avenue drums [of protest] separate from the belt-buckle tunes

5. Samuel A. Floyd, Jr., ed., *Black Music in the Harlem Renaissance* (New York, 1990), 4–5; Hazel Carby, *Reconstructing Womanhood: The Emergence of the Afro-American Woman Novelist* (New York, 1987), 164, 166, 165.

vibrating from pianos and spinning on every Victrola. Impossible" (59). And if there's anything we learn from Toni Morrison in our postcolonial times, it is that history is never over. Joe Trace, the New Negro who has transformed himself seven times, is unable to rid himself of the past that tracks him from Vesper County, Virginia, to New York City.

Characteristically, Morrison revises our conception of the New Negro by giving the title to Joe Trace, the door-to-door salesman of Cleopatra beauty products. Before Joe sells Cleopatra products, he works cleaning fish and toilets; his wife Violet does hair; their neighbor Malvonne cleans offices; even Alice Manfred works in the garment district. This movement away from the glamorous class of writers and musicians patronized by whites is central to her reclamation of the period known as the Jazz Age and the Harlem Renaissance. In *Jazz*, the male, middle-class New Negro is replaced by working-class men and women. Genteel, well-behaved Alice finds that she is also implicated in the loss and rage and appetite of the music, that she is not far removed from the embarrassing woman she calls "Violent." She is forced to recognize the humanity of Violet, a member of the black urban working class. Eventually the two women find a steadying companionship, each seeing in the other a reflection of her own grieved self. Together they contemplate the travails of black women: "Eating starch, choosing when to tackle the yoke, sewing, picking, cooking, chopping. Violet thought about it all and sighed. 'I thought it would be bigger than this. I knew it wouldn't last, but I did think it'd be bigger.'" Alice counters Violet's despair with a wisdom reminiscent of Violet's grandmother True Belle and *Beloved*'s Baby Suggs: "You got anything left to you to love, anything at all, do it. . . . Nobody's asking you to take it. I'm saying make it, make it!" (112–113). *Jazz* highlights the consciousness of black women's struggle to survive the violence of disenfranchisement reverberating across generations, across the North-South and rural-urban divide, a violence that is rendered in the elusive and mute figure of Wild. In *Jazz* as in *Beloved*, the history of economic oppression and racial violence is internalized, made visible in the interiority of lives lived within the dynamic allure of a restless city.

Just as the novel revises the image of the New Negro, it also revises the perception of the Jazz Age. In his account of jazz, James Collier notes, "Jazz criticism and jazz history have always concentrated on the big names, the stars, and the famous clubs and dance halls where they worked. In fact, jazz history is usually written around a chain of major figures—Oliver to Armstrong, to Beiderbecke, to Ellington, to Goodman, to Parker, to Davis, to Coltrane, to

Coleman—to the point where it might appear to the outsider that these great players *were* jazz history. But, in fact, perhaps ninety percent of the music has always been made by unknown players . . . for audiences drawn from the surrounding neighbourhood, town and county." He calls these unknown players "foot soldiers in the army," removed from the glamor of generals, and "the pure in heart" because they "are not playing jazz for fame and money, but sheerly because they love the music."[6] Toni Morrison's novel is partial to foot soldiers, minor players, the marginal musicians of history. The narrator of *Jazz* sings in praise of these local players of clarinets and horns, summoners of light, "pure and steady and kind of kind": "On the rooftops. Some on 254 where there is no protective railing; another at 131, the one with apple-green water-tank, and somebody right next to it, 133, where lard cans of tomato plants are kept, and a pallet for sleeping at night. . . . So from Lenox to . . . Eighth I could hear the men playing out their maple-sugar hearts, tapping it from four-hundred-year-old trees and letting it run down the trunk, wasting it because they didn't have a bucket to hold it and didn't want one either" (197).

The distinctive setting of the New Negro as Morrison contemplates this figure is the urban North; this is also the scene of jazz, which Richard Wright called "our wild, raw music," the "'spirituals' of the city pavements."[7] Morrison's *Jazz* pays homage to the urbanizing migrants who respond to the beguiling face of a city that enables the remaking of the self: "When [country people] fall in love with a city, it is forever. . . . There in the city they are not so much new as themselves: their stronger, riskier selves" (33). *Jazz* records the phenomena of the city seen from the eyes of country folk: "the way it's laid out for you, considerate, mindful of where you want to go and what you might need to-morrow" (9); it registers their "amazement of throwing open the window and being hypnotized for hours by people on the streets below" (34). The couple's train ride into the city captures the experience of "a million others" (32) : "They were hanging there, a young country couple, laughing and tapping back at the tracks" (30). The economic possibilities of the city are seen from the perspective of a rural culture: "White people literally threw money at you—just for being neighborly: opening a taxi door, picking up a package. And

6. James Lincoln Collier, *Jazz: The American Theme Song* (New York, 1993), 263–64, 75.
7. Richard Wright, *Twelve Million Black Voices* (New York, 1941), 128.

anything you had or made or found you could sell in the streets"; there was "more money than any of them had earned in one whole harvest" (106).

The anonymous narrator of *Jazz* recalls the *flaneur* (French for *city stroller*) whom Walter Benjamin invoked in his reading of Baudelaire's nineteenth-century Paris.[8] To the leisurely *flaneur*, the city reveals itself in its many capricious forms. The narrator in *Jazz*, captivated by the romance of the city, "watch[es] everything and everyone" (8): how the city ensouls people in its cityscape, creating an eros of its own where desire is "some combination of curved stone, and a swinging, high-heeled shoe moving in and out of sunlight." Itself the result of a collectivity, the city transforms individual consciousness, substituting vaster life processes with its own compelling ephemeras, "stars made irrelevant by the light of thrilling, wasteful lamps" (34). Appropriate to the urban spirit of jazz, the novel is interspersed with solos of pure *flanerie*: "I'm crazy about this City" (7); "I like the way the City makes people think they can do what they want and get away with it" for "it is there to back and frame you no matter what you do" (9). If the city shapes jazz, the music also impresses upon the city, for "the right tune . . . from the circles and grooves of a record could change the weather. From freezing to hot to cool" (51). It is this collective, interactive reciprocity of sight and sound, a shared space constituted by and constituting human behavior, that makes for the narrator's fascination with the city with a capital C.

The city in *Jazz* is not a space of alienation the way New York was for Son in *Tar Baby*. For the rural migrants at the turn of the century, the city is "thriftless, warm, scary and full of amiable strangers," a space that allows the formation of a collective consciousness (35). They could "feel themselves moving down the street among hundreds of others who moved the way they did, and who, when they spoke, regardless of the accent, treated language like the same intricate, malleable toy designed for their play" (32–33). The chief attribute of the city is that it marks the break from a repressive past: "Part of why they loved it was the specter they left behind" (33). It thus becomes a place of deliverance, the northern city being what the southern town of Palestine was not: the promised land. It is this context that explains why "the main tradition of black American literature has been persistently pro-urban in vision."[9] That the northern city delivers its own violence, that it is the place

8. Benjamin, *Illuminations*, 174.

9. Robert Butler and Yoshinobu Hakutani, eds., *The City in African American Literature* (Madison, Wis., 1995), 9.

of a dream deferred, does not negate the possibilities it offers. As the narrator remarks, "really there is no contradiction—rather it's a condition: the range of what an artful City can do" (118). *Jazz* represents both the real and false hopes offered by the city.

Though the city becomes a place to jettison the past, the past is much more than a piece of flotsam; the traumatic southern past has become somatic. Social injuries are embodied in those who leave the site of wreckage. Traumatic memories continue to exert themselves viscerally in involuntary acts of the body—such as Violet's sitting down in the street or Joe's tracking Dorcas. The past has constituted disturbances and hungers that will not go away in the city but that the city will augment in new ways, fostering a certain music; "just hearing it was like violating the law" (58). *Jazz* is about the violated ones driven to violate the law—the southern law that drives them out of rural homes in Rome, Troy, Vienna—imperial centers continuing the violent work of annexation and displacement in the United States. By violating the law, the characters impress upon us the violence that is not theirs alone.

The novel attempts to redefine the meaning and sensibility of the Jazz Age by aligning it to the experience of dispossession and the desires of the dispossessed. Like the city that generates it, the music "faked happiness, faked welcome" (59). Dispossession operates like a musical idea interwoven and rephrased by the various characters. For the characters of *Jazz*, it is not only the past that haunts—the present, too, is unsafe. The novel documents the terror of both the southern past and the northern present: "'Crackers in the South mad cause negroes were leaving; crackers in the North mad cause they were coming'" (128).

The novel offers a glimpse of the terror of the post-Reconstruction South that caused the historic migrations to the cities of the North. The Reconstruction era, from 1863 to 1877, gave way to one of the most repressive periods of white-black race relations, a period of social, political and economic terrorism carried out against freedmen and -women. It was the time of the Ku Klux Klan, lynching, denial of black suffrage backed by legal statute, and mob violence. It was the period of the Great Migration: "The wave of black people running from want and violence crested in the 1870s; the 1880s; the 1890s but was a steady stream in 1906 when Joe and Violet joined it." Among those who fled north were "the quiet children of the ones who had escaped from Springfield Ohio, Springfield Indiana, Greensburg Indiana, Wilmington Delaware, New

Orleans Louisiana, after raving whites had foamed all over the lanes and yards of home" (33). Joe Trace does not leave the South even after Vienna, his birthplace, is razed: "Red fire doing fast what white sheets took too long to finish: canceling every deed; vacating each and every field; emptying us out of our places so fast we went running from one part of the country to another." Joe Trace moves north after he is run off the land he has bought "'with two slips of paper [he] never saw nor signed'" (126). Then he becomes part of the black exodus from Vienna: "One week of rumors, two days of packing, and nine hundred Negroes, encouraged by guns and hemp, left Vienna, rode out of town on wagons or walked on their feet to who knew (or cared) where. With two days' notice? How can you plan where to go, and if you do know of a place you think will welcome you, where is the money to arrive?" (174). The reference to the exiled Jews underscores the oppression suffered by a people chosen and marked by the discourse of race. Enumerating the series of dispossessions and changes he has suffered, Joe Trace remarks wryly, "'You could say I've been a new Negro all my life'" (129).

As Richard Wright notes in *Twelve Million Black Voices*, "Only a few of those who dance and sing with us suspect the rawness of life out of which our laughing-crying tunes and quick dance-steps come; they do not know that our songs and dance are a banner of hope flung desperately up in the face of a world that has pushed us to the wall."[10] In *Jazz* we learn that underneath the busy days of the present, black women conceal sorrow and "the seep of rage. Molten. Thick and slow-moving." These are the women who dare not rest, who "fill their minds with soap and repair" because "a space of nothing to do would knock them down" (16). For Violet , the "globe light of the day" has "dark fissures," and "at the curve where the light stops . . . there is no foundation at all, but alleyways, crevices . . ." (22–23). The trauma that is Violet's is not hers alone: it is part of the troubled racial zeitgeist of the times, the music of the age. It is present in the "drums and the freezing faces" (54) in the silent protest march of July, 1917, "women and men marching down Fifth Avenue to advertise their anger over two hundred dead in East St. Louis" (57). These are the race riots that killed Dorcas' parents, Alice Manfred's sister and brother-in-law. It is Dorcas's aunt, stable and of middle-class propriety, who connects this desperation with jazz, the "lowdown music" she mistrusts, songs "that used to start in the head and fill the heart" but had now "dropped on down, down to

10. Wright, *Twelve Million Black Voices*, 130.

places below the sash and the buckled belts" (56). But raunchiness is not the only score. The "complicated anger" in the music "did not make her feel generous." It made Alice Manfred "hold her hand in the pocket of her apron to keep from smashing it through the glass pane to snatch the world in her fist and squeeze the life out of it for doing what it did and did and did to her and everybody else she knew or knew about" (59).

The drums Alice hears at the Fifth Avenue protest march perform a cognitive function in her understanding of her world and also serve as a metaphor for the novel's commitment to imagining a community. On the street Alice picked up a leaflet, "read the words and looked at Dorcas. . . . Some great gap lunged between the print and the child. She glanced between them struggling for the connection, something to close the distance between the silent staring child and the slippery crazy words. Then suddenly, like a rope cast for rescue, the drums spanned the distance, gathering them all up and connected them: Alice, Dorcas, her sister and brother-in-law, the Boy Scouts and the frozen black faces, the watchers on the pavement and those in the windows above" (58). *Jazz* also spans the distance, also connects. Rescuing from incomprehensibility the lived meaning of history not found in print reportage, the novel strains to gather in the rhythms of a jazz narrative the experience of a black collectivity.

Jazz is defined as a music that is "vocal and instrumental, monodic and polyphonic, individual and collective, improvised and worked out." The same may be said for the novel, in which, as in the music, "the artful handling of dissonance [is] an indication of mature artistry." Jazz scholar Paul Berliner observes that the music of jazz comes from "the singing and verbalizing mind" and depends on "the ability of an instrumentalist to perform with all the nuance of the voice." Berliner links jazz and storytelling by showing how musicians adopt metaphors of storytelling to convey the meaning of jazz oratory. He notes Paul Wertico's advice to his students that in initiating a solo they should think in terms of developing specific "characters and a plot": "You introduce these little different things that can be brought back out later on; and the way you put them together makes a little story. That can be [on the scale of] a sentence or a paragraph. . . . The real great cats can write novels." And, we might say, the real great cats of literature can make music. Morrison made a statement in 1983 that anticipated *Jazz:* "I think about what black writers do as having a quality of hunger and disturbance that never ends. Classical music satisfies and closes. Black music does not do that. Jazz always keeps you on the edge. There is no final chord. . . . There is always something else that you want from the music." Some reviewers of *Jazz* seem to want more from it, too. Paul Skenazy notes, "there is a hermetic feeling to the whole of too much suggested and implied, not enough presented." Camille Howard has called it a novel in which "nothing happens": "replete with richly etched portraits of desperately sad people and a whirlwind of historical events, *Jazz* remains curiously static, even icy. Its centrifugal force exerts compelling political energy, but it has little emotional center. . . . At the end of *Jazz* we are left with a stubborn, enduring marriage between two old people, a dead girl, a voyeuristic narrator who may have misinterpreted the entire thing, and a cruelly racist society."[11]

Like the musicians she emulates, Morrison taps a reservoir of feeling that demands of the reader/listener a cognitive and emotional attunement. *Jazz* is alternately hot and cool and not in a hurry to go anywhere; eventually it does. But like the music, it aims to find the groove of its own theme. Consider the notion of a groove from the musician's point of view: "'I don't care what kind of style a group plays as long as they settle into a groove where the rhythm keeps building instead of changing around,' Lou Donaldson asserts. 'It's like the way an African hits a drum. He hits it a certain way, and after a period of time, you feel it more than you did when he first started. He's playing the same thing, but the quality is different—it's settled into a groove.'"[12] The novel plays the same thing—the theme of dispossession—in different ways, and it demands of the listener a certain concentration. It has absorbed an entire social and political history within its pages and interprets it for us in a highly complex improvisation.

In the triad of Joe, Violet, and Dorcas, dispossession becomes a tonal idea that the rest of the characters repeat with variations. Just as in a jazz composition "harmonic qualities [suggest] linkages with particular harmonic synonyms, rhythmic elements evoking other patterns with similar configurations," the novel's discordant notes of loss build an architectonics whereby each story links with another.[13] Like the character Henry LesTroy, the hunter's hunter, the

---

11. Andre Hodeir, *Jazz: Its Evolution and Essence*, trans. David Noakes (New York, 1956), 240; Berliner, *Thinking in Jazz*, 208, 255; 202, 252; Toni Morrison, interview with Nellie McKay, *Contemporary Literature*, XXIII (1983), 429; Paul Skenazy, "Manhattan Music," San Francisco *Chronicle*, April 12, 1992, pp. 1, 11; Camille Howard, "Blues for Toni Morrison," *Express Books* (June, 1992), 1, 8–9.

12. Lou Donaldson, qtd. in Berliner, *Thinking in Jazz*, 349.

13. *Ibid.*, 194–95.

reader of *Jazz* must develop an "expertise in reading trails" that connect the stories of missing mothers, phantom fathers, amputated arms seeking other arms (148).

At the nexus of this history of loss lies the "cult of true womanhood" that Morrison explicates with reference to Violet's grandmother True Belle and her mistress Vera Louise Gray (*vera*, Latin for *true*). Hazel Carby summarizes the cult of true womanhood as the dominant ideology that set "the boundaries of acceptable female behavior from the 1820s until the Civil War"; it valorized "piety, purity, submissiveness and domesticity" as desirable virtues of the southern lady. Vera Louise's secret liason with Henry LesTroy in 1855 crosses the line of racial purity critical to the maintenance of the plantocracy. Carby observes, "Within the economic, political, and social system of slavery, women were at the nexus of its reproduction." White women "of the elite planter class . . . were viewed as the means of consolidation of property through the marriages of alliance between plantation families, and they gave birth to the inheritors of that property."[14] For not conforming to this role, Vera Louise Gray is wrathfully excommunicated by her parents. Morrison gives us a glimpse of what is at stake for Vera's father, Colonel Wordsworth Gray: "Realizing the terrible thing that had happened to his daughter made him sweat, for there were seven mulatto children on his land" (141). The offspring of the master and the enslaved black woman followed the condition of the mother and remained as slaves. If the seven mulatto children are visible markers of the contradictory standards of plantation patriarchy, the mulatto child of a white woman exposed an even greater contradiction.

In giving the name True Belle to the black woman, Morrison calls attention to the very different relationships black and white women had to antebellum southern patriarchy and to the power differential between a mistress and her slave. As a daughter of the planter class, Vera Louise could still inherit a slave: the twenty-seven-year-old True Belle "was the one she wanted and the one she took" (141). True Belle gives "her whole well life" to Vera Louise in Baltimore, raising her son Golden Gray, who has no idea of his father or of having usurped the place of Rose Dear, the daughter True Belle abandons in order to look after him. Golden Gray also does not know that he is the subject of the stories True Belle tells her granddaughter Violet, creating in her a longing to *be* him. No

14. Carby, *Reconstructing Womanhood*, 23–25.

wonder the narrator portrays Golden Gray in ironic terms: as a clueless dandy in a two-seat phaeton with his trunk of fineries, off to hunt his father. What's more, the estranged black father, Henry LesTroy ("Hunter"), and golden son meet only to witness, in Wild's giving birth to Joe, the estrangement of another mother and child. Violet and Joe are thus linked even before they meet; Violet's grandmother's beautiful ward, Golden Gray, has touched Joe's mother, Wild. Decades later, fair-skinned Dorcas will animate the abandoned child in Joe and will recall the golden child of Violet's dreams, drawing unconscious desire and resentment from both. If Dorcas is linked both to Wild and to Golden Gray, Wild literally carries the traces of Vera Louise and her son. In the cave where Wild is both present and absent, Joe Trace finds objects that belong to Vera and Golden Gray: a green dress, a set of silver brushes and a silver cigar case, a silk shirt. Thus the secret cave situated beside the Treason River becomes the matrix of a history of maternal loss that can be traced back to the cult of true womanhood.

It is both befitting and ironic that the articulation of parental loss is given to Golden Gray—the child pampered by Vera Louise and True Belle—as he waits for his phantom father to appear. His pain serves to highlight the loss of those who received neither maternal nor parental love, such as Joe and Violet. Golden Gray describes the loss in visceral terms as the amputation of an arm: "I don't need the arm. But I do need to know what it could have been like to have had it. . . . This part of me that does not know me, has never touched me or lingered at my side. This gone-away hand that never helped me over the stile, or . . . stroked my hair, fed me food" (158). In this soliloquy, Golden Gray also articulates the novel's stance toward its own material: "I am not going to . . . find the arm that was removed from me. I am going to freshen the pain, point it, so we both know what it is for. . . . I will locate it so the severed part can remember the snatch, the slice of its disfigurement. Perhaps then the arm will no longer be a phantom, but will take its own shape, grow its own muscle and bone, and its blood will pump from the loud singing that has found the purpose of its serenade. Amen" (158–59).

Like jazz, the novel builds upon the idiom of the blues. *Jazz* is about need and love and the ways history specifies and twists the expressions of these universals: the child's need for the love of a parent, the adolescent's yearning, the adult's longing. All three characters in the troubled triad of need and longing—Violet, Joe, and Dorcas—have lost their mothers to racial violence. Violet's mother, Rose Dear, never recovers from the dispossession of her house and land; separated earlier from her mother and later from her activist husband (who must run for his life), she commits suicide by jumping into a well. Violet is the daughter who will not be a mother because she does not want to reproduce the condition of her mother or herself. But childlessness comes to haunt her, "mother-hunger" wearing her down after age forty, so she ends up sleeping with a doll, almost stealing a baby, and finding in Dorcas and then Felice traces of her own might-have-been daughter.

In the figures of Rose Dear and Wild, the novel represents the terror and bewilderment of black maternal experience during slavery and its aftermath. The psychic devastation is passed on to the next generation. Wild bequeaths Joe an "inside nothing," leaving him to seek traces of herself in the fields of Vienna and the streets of New York City (37). Joe is faced with the impossibility of tracking the mother who is present only in her absence. This impossible condition is the founding of his love for Dorcas, of a blind and blinding instinct enacting oedipal desire. However, Joe's is not the universal oedipal story of Freud's Vienna; the configurations of his desire are specific to the Vienna of the racialized South. He is doomed to reenact through Dorcas the narcissistic wound inflicted by the mother, whose agency in this regard is absent; herself a history of woundedness, Wild is the wound and treason of history that bore him.

An orphaned survivor of the East St. Louis race riots, Dorcas loses her father when he is "pulled off a streetcar and stomped to death" (57); her mother burns in their torched house. Longing to be "enclosed in arms, and supported by the core of the world," her "hunger" matches Joe's (63). Each carries "an inside nothing" that they recognize in each other and fill (37). Dorcas embodies the traumatized survivor's secret impulse to die—she does not struggle to live when she is shot. As Cathy Caruth observed of modern trauma theory, "the postulation of a drive to death" implies recognition of "the destructive force that the violence of history imposes on the human psyche"; it views "the formation of history as the endless repetition of previous violence."[15] Dorcas's death would certainly uphold such a view of the past. The third day of the new year of 1926, which begins with death, recalls Shadrack's National Suicide Day in *Sula* and supports the narrator's conviction that "the past was an abused record with no choice but to repeat itself at the crack" (220).

However, while Dorcas is sacrificed to a history repeating itself, the trauma

15. Caruth, *Unclaimed Experience*, 63.

of history is prevented from being all-consuming; this is the "grace note" offered in the concluding chapter of *Jazz*. By the novel's end, the wounded triad of Violet, Joe, and Dorcas—a configuration of unworked-through trauma—is replaced with the healing threesome of Violet, Joe, and Felice. Nobody shoots anybody; the narrator's prediction is wrong. True to the spirit of jazz, the characters are bound yet have space in which to improvise and to go ahead of the beat. But by then we have heard the protest—"the pervading ache of freedom"—in the solos, duets, and trios of desire: "What's the world for if you can't make it up the way you want it?" (208).

In *Jazz*, history is more like an unfinished plot that must work itself out in the life of the present; as such the novel is in many ways the denouement of *Beloved*. The cross-generational pain of slavery and its brutal aftermath in the emancipated and reconstructed South of the 1890s is palpable in the lives of all the characters. In *Beloved*, the chief metaphor is that of spirit possession, of haunting; in *Jazz*, the metaphor is of hunting. The metaphor of tracks and trails, hunters and quarry construe the present as tracked or hunted by the past. The figure of Beloved from the previous novel merges with the figure of Wild, amplifying the haunting tracks of a jazz record, spinning the characters to its own circles of hunger and thwarted desire.

Jazz overlaps with *Beloved* and takes off where it stops. *Beloved* opens in 1873 with Sethe and Denver's haunting by Beloved and ends in the same year with Beloved's leaving: "Disappeared, some say, exploded right before their very eyes. Ella is not sure. 'Maybe,' she says, 'maybe not. Could be hiding in the trees for another chance.'" The last we see of her before she vanishes, Beloved is standing naked, "thunderblack and glistening," "her belly big and tight."[16] In *Jazz* in the year 1873, Golden Gray sees "in the trees . . . a naked, berry-black woman. As soon as she sees him, she starts then turns suddenly to run. . . . Her terror is so great her body flees before her eyes are ready to find the route of escape" (144). Wild's reaction to Golden Gray is similar to Beloved's reaction to white men; recall Beloved's terror of "men without skin." It is tempting to follow the trails Morrison has left between the two novels. Is the woman called Wild with "that babygirl laugh" Beloved? Hunter's Hunter thinks her dead, but "it saddened him to learn that instead of resting she was hungry still"; the connection to Beloved is again evoked in this reference to hunger. "She was still out there—and real" (167). However, this is not the

16. Morrison, *Beloved*, 263, 261.

story of Beloved as Wild, "powerless, invisible, wastefully daft"; this is a son's story. It is about how a mother's absence and presence "everywhere and no-where" (179) haunts him: "All in all, [Joe] made three solitary journeys to find her. In Vienna he had lived first with the fear of her, then the joke of her, finally the obsession, followed by rejection of her" (175). The site of her presence/absence is symbolic: a rock cave beside a river called Treason where "the ground was as porous as a seive. A step could swallow your foot or your whole self" (182). The woman/mother lives in a womblike formation in the earth, a matrix that Joe is forever seeking to enter and emerge from. In his exploratory motions, Joe mimes the birth process, "crawling, squirming through a space low enough to graze his hair . . . he pulled himself all the way out to reenter head first" (183). Joe's obsession with his mother—"But where is *she?*" (184)—becomes transferred to an obsession with Dorcas, yielding to "There she is" (187). Decades after he has given up following his mother's trail, the track begins to speak; only now, by transference, the hunted is Dorcas. Dorcas's "sugar-flawed skin, the high wild bush the bed pillows made of her hair," links her to Wild, who moved in the tall sugarcane and the bush (28). When Dorcas leaves him in preference for a younger man, Joe Trace lives again the primary betrayal of his life by shooting the treason of history.

The conclusion to Joe and Violet's story invokes the ending of *Beloved,* when Paul D "wants to put his story next to [Sethe's]." Both couples share a hard-won love whose chief attribute is having endured the buffetings of re-pressed memory. Both *Beloved* and *Jazz* take the difficult material of a collective trauma and transform it into an encounter whereby the narrative becomes a "medium of historical transmission" and "the unsuspected medium of a heal-ing."[17]

Jazz offers healing to those who survive the violent confrontation with the repressed past. Spring comes to the city with fresh life. With help from Alice Manfred, Violet is no longer dissociated from herself: she is no longer troubled by the Violet who knifes a dead girl. After a period of deep mourning, Joe is no longer doomed to track what he cannot have. Felice, unlike Dorcas, does not have to become anybody's "alibi or hammer or toy" (222). The narrator, though self-confessedly out of touch with her characters' lives, is in touch with the one figure everyone else was not—Wild, the bewildered figure of the past

---

17. Morrison, *Beloved,* 273; Felman, *Trauma: Explorations in Memory,* ed. Caruth, 20.

whom it is the narrator's mission to summon. "She has seen me and is not afraid of me. She hugs me. Understands me. Has given me her hand. I am touched by her. Released in secret" (221). What's more, as the narrator reminds us, our own hands are upon the text: "Look where your hands are. Now" (229). It is this laying on of hands, hands bearing witness and healing, that the past demands and *Jazz* invites. Laying our hands on the past so that it may be delivered: "make me, remake me," says the narrative voice, as if acknowledging the therapeutic nature of the encounter.

If knowing is embodied in the metaphor of grasping, the narrator of *Jazz* plays upon that metaphor—on what can be grasped and what cannot. The narrator confesses she cannot seem to grasp that her traumatized characters have survived the double plot of destruction—both the destructive plot of history and her own narrative plottings of fatal pain. In eluding her, they are also luckily eluding the deterministic cycle of history, which is shown to be open to improvisation. But in their very survival they have traced the generational violence of a history that must be grasped by the reader.

The last chapter of *Jazz* is a narrative sleight of hand in which the narrator/composer confesses incompetence as an improviser. "I got so aroused while meddling, while finger-shaping, I overreached and missed the obvious." The narrator had predicted the repetition of violence because she was sure "the past was an abused record with no choice but to repeat itself at the crack." Instead, the characters were "busy being original, complicated, changeable" (220). As James Collier points out, "One of the worst accusations that can be flung at a [jazz] musician by other musicians is that 'he doesn't listen.' The unwillingness to take into account what everybody else is doing is taken as arrogance, a mark of disrespect for one's fellow players, and is seen as damaging the music." The narrator's misinterpretation of the unfolding narrative turns into a "musical save"—the jazz convention of "resolving the disparity between musical intention and realization in performance." Furthermore, as Berliner notes, sometimes a save is effected by responding to the false note by giving the piece "a new melodic twist."[18] Just as the deviation from the intended notes leads to the improvising of a new maneuver, the narrator of *Jazz* saves the situation by turning it into a metanarrative confession of the desire to tell and of her own role as omniscient narrator: "Pain. I seem to have an affection, a kind of sweettooth for it. Bolts of lightning, little rivulets of thunder. And I the eye of

18. Collier, *Jazz*, 52; Berliner, *Thinking in Jazz*, 210–16

the storm. Mourning the split trees, hens starving on rooftops. Figuring out what can be done to save them since they cannot save themselves without me because—well, it's my storm isn't it? I break lives to prove I can mend them back again. . . . I am uneasy now. Feeling a bit false. What, I wonder, what would I be without a few brilliant spots of blood to ponder? Without aching words that set, then miss, the mark?"(219). If the novel's singular focus has been on showing the damage of history, such a confession makes way for the possibilities of overcoming the damage. Such an admission makes space for narrative reparation.

From the characters' perspective, she admits she is the classic unreliable narrator whose point of view is partial: "They knew how little I could be counted on. . . ." She humanizes the role of the narrator as someone vulnerable and controling, insightful and blind, "thinking [her] space, [her] view was the only one that was or that mattered" (220). She has evinced such self-reflexive scruples before; she has broken the omniscient narrator's code by verbalizing her own partisan envisioning of Golden Gray: "What was I thinking of? How could I have imagined him so poorly? Not noticed the hurt that was not linked to the color of his skin, or the blood that beat beneath it. But to some other thing that longed for authenticity" (160). *Jazz* is self-conscious about the capacity of art to mediate in its time and space the desires of historic subjects.

The novel ends with a finale of writerly/readerly desire. Having failed to grasp Joe and Violet—and this is a victory for the characters who escape the plot of history—the narrator is finally left alone with the reader, in whose presence she has tried to grasp the past. The reader, in turn, has tried to grasp her narrative. This mutual coming-to-grasp is celebrated in amorous terms as the aligning of two who together make sense of the solitary acts of writing and reading. The intimate voice of the narrator is embodied in the book we hold in our hands. Witness this Whitmanesque declaration of secret love addressed to the reader of *Jazz*:

That I love the way you hold me, how close you let me be to you. I like your fingers on and on, lifting and turning. I have watched your face for a long time now, and missed your eyes when you went away from me. Talking to you and hearing you answer—that's the kick.

But I can't say that aloud; I can't tell anyone that I have been waiting for this all my life and that being chosen to wait is the reason I can. If I were able I'd say it. Say make me, remake me. You are free to do it and I am free to let you because look, look. Look where your hands are. Now. (229)

This passage anticipates the call-and-response statement made by the griot to her listeners in Morrison's Nobel Prize acceptance speech of 1993: "Look how lovely it is, this thing we have done—together."[19] "Make me, remake me," urges the narrative voice and the book. The narrator's plea/permission is an acknowledgement of the reader's agency in producing the text's meaning, of the reader's intimate role as witness/participant in a therapeutic encounter. But more, in the reader's alleged freedom to make, remake is a gentle reminder of the responsibility of remaking the social text, of bringing the reader to the task of the present. Now.

19. Morrison, *The Nobel Lecture*, 30.

SELECTED BIBLIOGRAPHY

Achebe, Chinua. *Hopes and Impediments: Selected Essays.* New York, 1988.

————. *Morning Yet on Creation Day: Essays.* Garden City, N.Y., 1975.

Allen, Robert. *Black Awakening in Capitalist America.* Garden City, N.Y., 1970.

Anchor, Robert. "Bakhtin's Truths of Laughter." *Clio,* XIV (1985), 237–57.

Anderson, Benedict. *Imagined Communities: Reflections on the Origin and Spread of Nationalism.* New York, 1983.

Anderson, Linda. "The Re-Imagining of History in Contemporary Women's Fiction." In *Plotting Change: Contemporary Women's Fiction,* edited by Linda Anderson, 129–41. London, 1990.

Andrews, William L. *To Tell a Free Story: The First Century of Afro-American Autobiography, 1760–1865.* Urbana, Il., 1986.

Angelo, Bonnie. "The Pain of Being Black." *Time,* May 22, 1989, pp. 120–23.

Antze, Paul and Michael Lambek, eds. *Tense Past: Cultural Essays in Trauma and Memory.* New York, 1996.

Appiah, K. A., and Henry Louis Gates, Jr., eds. *Toni Morrison: Critical Perspectives Past and Present.* New York, 1993.

Armstrong, Paul B. *Conflicting Readings: Variety and Validity in Interpretation.* Chapel Hill, N.C., 1990.

Ashcroft, Bill, Gareth Griffiths, and Helen Tiffin. *The Empire Writes Back: Theory and Practice in Post-Colonial Literatures.* London, 1989.

Awkward, Michael. *Inspiriting Influences: Tradition, Revision, and Afro-American Women's Novels.* New York, 1989.

Baker, Houston. *Blues, Ideology and Afro-American Literature: A Vernacular Theory.* Chicago, 1985.

Bakhtin, Mikhail. *The Dialogic Imagination: Four Essays.* Austin, 1981.

————. *Rabelais and His World.* Translated by Helene Iswolsky. Bloomington, Ind., 1984.

Baldwin, James. *Notes of a Native Son.* Boston, 1955.

Barrett, Michele. "Ideology and the Cultural Production of Gender." In *Feminist Criticism and Social Change: Sex, Class, and Race in Literature and Culture,* edited by Judith Newton and Deborah Rosenfelt, 65–85. New York, 1985.

Benjamin, Walter. *Illuminations.* Translated by Harry Zohn, edited by Hannah Arendt. New York, 1968.

Bennett, Lerone, Jr. *Before the Mayflower: A History of Black America*. Chicago, 1969.
———. *The Challenge of Blackness*. Chicago, 1972.
Berger, John. *Ways of Seeing*. Harmondsworth, Eng., 1977.
Berliner, Paul F. *Thinking in Jazz: The Infinite Art of Improvisation*. Chicago, 1994.
Bhabha, Homi. "Of Mimicry and Man: The Ambivalence of Colonial Discourse." *October*, XXVIII (1984), 125–33.
———, ed. *Nation and Narration*. London, 1990.
Blake, Susan. "Folklore and Community in Song of Solomon." *MELUS*, VII (Fall, 1980), 77–82.
Bloom, Harold, ed. *Toni Morrison*. New York, 1990.
Brathwaite, Edward. *Mother Poem*. Oxford, Eng., 1977.
Braxton, Joanne M., and Andrée Nicola McLaughlin, eds. *Wild Women in the Whirlwind: Afra-American Culture and the Contemporary Literary Renaissance*. New Brunswick, N.J., 1990.
Brennan, Timothy. *Salman Rushdie and the Third World: Myths of the Nation*. New York, 1989.
Butler, Robert James. "Open Movement and Selfhood in Toni Morrison's *Song of Solomon*." *Centennial Review*, XXVIII–XXIX (1984–85), 58–75.
Butler, Robert, and Yoshinobu Hakutani, eds. *The City in African-American Literature*. Madison, Wis., 1995.
Butler-Evans, Elliott. *Race, Gender, and Desire: Narrative Strategies in the Fiction of Toni Cade Bambara, Toni Morrison, and Alice Walker*. Philadelphia, 1989.
Cade, Toni, ed. *The Black Woman*. New York, 1970.
Carby, Hazel. *Reconstructing Womanhood: The Emergence of the Afro-American Woman Novelist*. New York, 1987.
Caruth, Cathy. *Unclaimed Experience: Trauma, Narrative, and History*. Baltimore, 1996.
———, ed. *Trauma: Explorations in Memory*. Baltimore, 1995.
Certeau, Michel de. *Heterologies: Discourse on the Other*. Translated by Brian Massumi. Minneapolis, Minn., 1986.
Chatterjee, Partha. *Nationalist Thought and the Colonial World: A Derivative Discourse*. Minneapolis, Minn. 1986.
Cherniavsky, Eva. "Subaltern Studies in a U.S. Frame." *Boundary 2*, XXIII (Summer, 1996), 85–110.
Christian, Barbara. *Black Women Novelists: The Development of a Tradition, 1892–1976*. Westport, Conn., 1980.
———. *Black Feminist Criticism: Perspectives on Black Women Writers*. New York, 1985.
Cixous, Helene. "The Laugh of the Medusa." *Signs* (Summer, 1976), 281–82.
Collier, James Lincoln. *Jazz: The American Theme Song*. New York, 1993.
Collins, Patricia Hill. *Black Feminist Thought: Knowledge, Consciousness, and the Politics of Empowerment*. Boston, 1990.
Cruse, Harold. *Rebellion or Revolution?* New York, 1968.
Davis, Angela. *Women, Race and Class*. New York, 1981.
Davis, Charles, and Henry Louis Gates, Jr., eds. *The Slave's Narrative*. New York, 1985.

Davis, Cynthia. "Self, Society, and Myth in Toni Morrison's Fiction." *Contemporary Literature*, XXIII (1982), 323–42.

Deleuze, Gilles, and Felix Guattari. *Kafka: Toward a Minor Literature*. Translated by Dana Polan. Minneapolis, Minn. 1987.

Dhareshwar, Vivek. "Toward a Narrative Epistemology of the Postcolonial Predicament." *Inscriptions*, V (1989), 135–57.

Dirlik, Arif. "Culturalism as Hegemonic Ideology and Liberating Practice." *Cultural Critique*, VI (Spring, 1987), 13–50.

Dubey, Madhu. *Black Women Novelists and the Nationalist Aesthetic*. Bloomington, Ind., 1994.

Du Bois, W. E. B. *The Souls of Black Folk*. New York, 1969.

Eagleton, Terry. *Ideology: An Introduction*. New York, 1991.

———. *Marxism and Literary Criticism*. Berkeley, 1976.

———. "Nationalism: Irony and Commitment." *Nationalism, Colonialism and Literature: Terry Eagleton, Fredric Jameson, Edward Said*. Minneapolis, Minn., 1990.

Eliot, T. S. "The Waste Land." *Selected Poems*. London, 1976.

Ellison, Ralph. *Invisible Man*. New York, 1952.

Falk, Marcia. *Love Lyrics from the Bible: A Translation and Literary Study of the Song of Songs*. Sheffield, Eng., 1982.

Fanon, Frantz. *The Wretched of the Earth*. Translated by Constance Farrington. New York, 1965.

Felman, Shoshana, and Dori Laub, eds. *Testimony: Crises of Witnessing in Literature, Psychoanalysis, and History*. New York, 1991.

Floyd, Samuel A., Jr., ed. *Black Music in the Harlem Renaissance*. New York, 1990.

Foster, Frances Smith, ed. *A Brighter Coming Day: A Frances Ellen Watkins Harper Reader*. New York, 1990.

Freud, Sigmund. "Mourning and Melancholia." *On Metapsychology*. Vol. XI of Freud, *The Pelican Freud Library*. Harmondsworth, 1964.

Gates, Henry Louis, Jr., ed. *Black Literature and Literary Theory*. New York, 1984.

———, ed. *Reading Black, Reading Feminist: A Critical Anthology*. New York, 1990.

Georgia Writers Project. *Drums and Shadows*. Westport, Conn., 1976.

Giddings, Paula. *When and Where I Enter: The Impact of Black Women on Race and Sex in America*. New York, 1984.

Goldman, Anne E. "I Made the Ink: (Literary) Production and Reproduction in *Dessa Rose* and *Beloved*." *Feminist Studies*, XVI (1990), 313–30.

Gramsci, Antonio. *Antonio Gramsci: Selections from Political Writings 1910–1920*. Translated by John Matthews. New York, 1977.

Griffin, Farah Jasmine. *'Who Set You Flowin'?' The African American Migration Narrative*. New York, 1995.

Hanchard, Michael. "Identity, Meaning, and the African American." *Social Text*, XXIV (1990), 31–42.

Harper, Frances. *Iola Leroy*. Boston, 1987.

Hayden, Robert. *Angle of Ascent: New and Selected Poems*. New York, 1975.

Harris, Wilson. *Womb of Space: The Cross-Cultural Imagination*. Westport, Conn., 1983.

Herndl, Diane Price, and Robyn Warhol, eds. *Feminisms: An Anthology of Literary Theory and Criticism*. New Brunswick, N.J., 1991.

Hogue, W. Lawrence. *Race, Modernity, Postmodernity: A Look at the History and the Literatures of People of Color Since the 1960s*. Albany, N.Y., 1996.

Holloway, Karla F. C. *Moorings and Metaphors: Figures of Culture and Gender in Black Women's Literature*. New Brunswick, N.J., 1992.

hooks, bell. *Talking Back: Thinking Feminist, Thinking Black*. Boston, 1989.

Hughes, Langston. *Selected Poems of Langston Hughes*. New York, 1974.

Irigaray, Luce. *This Sex Which Is Not One*. Ithaca, N.Y., 1985.

Jacobs, Harriet A. *Incidents in the Life of a Slave Girl*. New York, 1973.

Jameson, Fredric. *The Political Unconscious: Narrative as a Socially Symbolic Act*. Ithaca, N.Y., 1981.

JanMohamed, Abdul R. *Manichean Aesthetics: The Politics of Literature in Colonial Africa*. Amherst, Mass., 1983.

JanMohamed, Abdul, and David Lloyd, eds. *The Nature and Context of Minority Discourse*. New York, 1990.

Jones, Bessie W., and Audrey L. Vinson. *The World of Toni Morrison: Explorations in Literary Criticism*. Dubuque, Iowa, 1985.

Jones, LeRoi. *Blues People*. New York, 1963.

Jung, Carl Gustav. *The Archetypes and the Collective Unconscious*. Princeton, 1959.

Kernan, Alvin. *The Death of Literature*. New Haven, 1990.

Koller, Alice. *The Stations of Solitude*. New York, 1990.

LaCapra, Dominick. *Representing the Holocaust: History, Theory, Trauma*. Ithaca, N.Y., 1994.

———, ed. *The Bounds of Race: Perspectives on Hegemony and Resistance*. Ithaca, N.Y., 1991.

Lamming, George. *The Pleasures of Exile*. London, 1984.

Landry, Donna, and Gerald MacLean. *Materialist Feminisms*. Cambridge, Mass., 1993.

Lee, Dorothy H. "Song of Solomon: To Ride The Air." *BALF*, XVI (Summer, 1982), 64–70.

Levine, George, ed. *Aesthetics and Ideology*. New Brunswick, N.J., 1994.

Malcolm X. *Malcolm X on Afro-American History*. New York, 1970.

Marshall, Paule. *Praisesong for the Widow*. New York, 1983.

Mbalia, Doreatha Drummond. *Toni Morrison's Developing Class Consciousness*. London, 1991.

McClintock, Anne. "The Angel of Progress: Pitfalls of the Term 'Postcolonialism.'" In *Colonial Discourse/Postcolonial Theory*, edited by Francis Barker, Peter Hulme, and Margaret Iversen, 253–66. Manchester, Eng., 1994.

McKay, Nellie, ed. *Critical Essays on Toni Morrison*. Boston, 1988.

Minh-ha, Trinh T. "Not You/Like You: Postcoloniality and the Interlocking Questions of Identity and Difference." *Inscriptions*, III–IV (1988), 71–77.

————. *Woman, Native, Other: Writing Postcoloniality and Feminism.* Bloomington, Ind., 1989.

Mobley, Marilyn Sanders. *Folk Roots and Mythic Wings in Sarah Orne Jewett and Toni Morrison: The Cultural Function of Narrative.* Baton Rouge, 1991.

Mohanty, Satya. "The Epistemic Status of Cultural Identity: On *Beloved* and the Postcolonial Condition." *Cultural Critique,* XXIV (Spring, 1993), 41–80.

Moi, Toril, ed. *The Kristeva Reader.* New York, 1986.

Morrison, Toni. *Beloved.* New York, 1987.

————. *The Bluest Eye.* New York, 1970.

————. "City Limits, Village Values: Concepts of the Neighborhood in Black Fiction." In *Literature and Urban Experience,* edited by Michael C. Jaye and Ann Chalmer Watts, 35–43. New Brunswick, N.J., 1981.

————. *Jazz.* New York, 1992.

————. *The Nobel Lecture in Literature, 1993.* New York, 1994.

————. *Playing in the Dark: Whiteness and the Literary Imagination.* Cambridge, Mass., 1992.

————. "Rediscovering Black History." *New York Times Magazine,* August 11, 1974, pp. 16, 18.

————. "Rootedness: The Ancestor as Foundation." In *Black Women Writers (1950–1980): A Critical Evaluation,* edited by Mari Evans, 339–45. Garden City, N.Y., 1984.

————. "The Site of Memory." In *Inventing the Truth: The Art and Craft of Memoir,* edited by William Zinsser, 103–24. Boston, 1987.

————. *Song of Solomon.* New York, 1977.

————. *Sula.* New York, 1973.

————. *Tar Baby.* New York, 1981.

————. "Unspeakable Things Unspoken: The Afro-American Presence in American Literature." *Michigan Quarterly Review,* XXVIII (1989), 1–34.

————. "What the Black Woman Thinks About Women's Lib." *New York Times Magazine,* August 22, 1971, p. 15.

————, ed. *Race-ing Justice, En-Gendering Power: Essays on Anita Hill, Clarence Thomas, and the Construction of Social Reality.* New York, 1992.

Morrison, Toni, and Claudia Brodsky Lacour, eds. *Birth of a Nation'hood: Gaze, Script, and Spectacle in the O. J. Simpson Case.* New York, 1997.

Mukerji, Chandra, and Michael Schudson, eds. *Rethinking Popular Culture: Contemporary Perspectives in Cultural Studies.* Berkeley, 1991.

Naipaul, V. S. *The Mimic Men.* London, 1967.

Nandy, Ashis. *The Intimate Enemy: Loss and Recovery of Self Under Colonialism.* Delhi, India, 1983.

Neal, Larry. *Visions of a Liberated Future / Black Arts Movement Writings: Larry Neal,* edited by Michael Schwartz. New York, 1989.

Nasr, Seyyed Hossein. *Islamic Art and Spirituality.* Albany, N.Y., 1987.

Peterson, Nancy J., ed. "Toni Morrison Double Issue." *Modern Fiction Studies*, XXXIX (1993).

Radhakrishnan, R. "Nationalism, Gender, and the Narrative of Identity." In *Nationalisms and Sexualities*, edited by Andrew Parker, Mary Russo, Doris Sommer, and Patricia Yaeger, 77–95. New York, 1992.

Rampersad, Arnold, and Deborah E. McDowell, eds. *Slavery and the Literary Imagination*. Baltimore, 1989.

Rich, Adrienne. *Blood, Bread, and Poetry*. New York, 1986.

Rodman, Selden. "Whites and Blacks." *National Review*, June 26, 1981, pp. 730–32.

Roth, Michael. *The Ironist's Cage: Memory, Trauma, and the Construction of History*. New York, 1995.

Said, Edward. *Culture and Imperialism*. New York, 1993.

Samuels, Wilfred D., and Clenora Hudson-Weems. *Toni Morrison*. Boston, 1990.

Sangari, Kumkum. "Politics of the Possible." *Cultural Critique*, VII (Fall, 1987), 168.

Sangari, Kumkum, and Sudesh Vaid, eds. *Recasting Women: Essays in Colonial History*. New Delhi, India, 1989.

Sartre, Jean-Paul. *What Is Literature?* New York, 1966.

Scruggs, Charles. "The Nature of Desire in Toni Morrison's *Song of Solomon*." *Arizona Quarterly*, XXXVIII (Winter, 1982), 311–35.

Silko, Leslie Marmon. *Ceremony*. New York, 1977.

Slemon, Stephen. "Monuments of Empire: Allegory/Counter-Discourse/Post-Colonial Writing." *Kunapipi*, IX (1987), 1–16.

Smith, Barbara. "Toward a Black Feminist Criticism." In *Feminist Criticism and Social Change*, edited by Judith Newton and Deborah Rosenfelt, 3–17. New York, 1985.

Sollors, Werner. *Beyond Ethnicity: Consent and Descent in American Culture*. New York, 1986.

Spillers, Hortense, and Marjorie Pryse, eds. *Conjuring: Black Women, Fiction and Literary Tradition*. Bloomington, Ind., 1985.

Spivak, Gayatri Chakravorty. *The Post-Colonial Critic: Interviews, Strategies, Dialogues*. Edited by Sarah Harasym. New York, 1990.

———. "The Rani of Sirmur." In *Europe and its Others, Proceedings of the Essex Conference on the Sociology of Literature, July 1984*, edited by Francis Barker, *et al.*, 128–51. Vol. I of 2 vols. Colchester, Eng., 1985.

Steedman, Carolyn Kay. *Landscape for a Good Woman: A Story of Two Lives*. New Brunswick, N.J., 1987.

Tate, Claudia, ed. *Black Women Writers at Work*. New York, 1983.

Taylor-Guthrie, Danille, ed. *Conversations With Toni Morrison*. Jackson, Miss., 1994.

Tiffin, Helen. "Post-Colonialism, Post-Modernism and the Rehabilitation of Post-Colonial History." *Journal of Commonwealth Literature*, XXIII (1988), 169–81.

Turner, Victor. *Dramas, Fields, and Metaphors: Symbolic Action in Human Society*. Ithaca, N.Y., 1974.

Voloshinov, V. N. *Marxism and the Philosophy of Language*. Translated by Ladislav Matejka and I. R. Titunik. Cambridge, Mass., 1986.

Walker, Alice. "Everyday Use." In *In Love and Trouble*. New York, 1973.

———. *In Search of Our Mothers' Gardens*. New York, 1983.

Wall, Cheryl A., ed. *Changing Our Own Words: Essays on Criticism, Theory, and Writing by Black Women*. New Brunswick, N.J., 1989.

West, Cornel. "The New Cultural Politics of Difference." *October*, LIII (Summer, 1990).

———. *Race Matters*. Boston, 1993.

White, Hayden. *The Content of the Form: Narrative Discourse and Historical Representation*. Baltimore, 1987.

Williams, Raymond. *Marxism and Literature*. Oxford, Eng., 1977.

Willis, Susan. *Specifying: Black Women Writing the American Experience*. Madison, Wis., 1987.

Winant, Howard. "Postmodern Racial Politics in the United States: Difference and Inequality." *Socialist Review*, XX (January–March, 1990).

Woolf, Virginia. *Mrs. Dalloway*. London, 1925.

Wright, Richard. *Native Son*. New York, 1987.

———. *Twelve Million Black Voices*. New York, 1941.